C0-ARQ-636

MÈRE MARIE
OF THE URSULINES

BOOKS BY
AGNES REPPLIER

17320

BXQ
8026
.M3
R42

BX
4705
.M36
R4

Mère Marie of the Ursulines
A Study in Adventure
by AGNES REPPLIER, LITT D.

The Literary Guild of America
New York   MCMXXXI

ST. JOSEPH'S UNIVERSITY   STX
BXQ 8026 .M3 .R42
Mere Marie of the Ursulines,

3 9353 00016 6346

COPYRIGHT, 1931
BY AGNES REPPLIER
ALL RIGHTS RESERVED

FIRST EDITION

BX 4705
M13 6
co. 4

PRINTED AT THE *Country Life Press*, GARDEN CITY, N. Y., U. S. A.

CONTENTS

*Inscription and Seals Engraved on the Wall of the
Ursuline Convent in Quebec*

(Translation)

*On this site, given by the Company of New France
to the Ursulines who landed in Quebec in 1639,
was founded in 1641 a convent, destroyed by fire in
1650, and rebuilt in 1651.   There was erected also
a church, the cornerstone of which was laid by
M. de Lauzon.   It was burned in 1686, and rebuilt in 1720.   Here was laid the body of the
Marquis de Montcalm in 1759, and here was
celebrated the second centenary of the Feast of the
Sacred Heart in this convent.   The cornerstone of
the present church was laid August 28, 1901, by
Mgr. L.-N. Bégin, Archbishop of Quebec.*

Chapter I

SAINT URSULA AND THE URSULINES

OF COURSE the Ursulines were the most adventurous of nuns; they had the most adventurous of patronesses. Saints in plenty have gone on pilgrimages; but no other saint ever carried eleven thousand virgins along with her. Saints in plenty have been martyred; but no other saint ever shared martyrdom with eleven thousand companions. It was the noble amplitude of Saint Ursula's enterprise which gave vivacity to her legend, and distinction to her name.

Thirteen lines carved on a stone of unknown date afford the sole foundation for her story. They are called the Inscription of Clematius, and may be found in the choir of the Church of St. Ursula in Cologne. Clematius, a man of rank, built in the Fifth Century a basilica in honor of the virgin martyrs who met their deaths on that spot. So much may be deciphered from the stone; but not a great deal more, save that the basilica replaced a still older church which had fallen into ruins, and that all men were warned, under penalty of everlasting fire, against burying anyone who was not a virgin within the sacred walls. In no liturgy earlier than the Ninth Century is there any mention of these martyrs. The number first given is eleven, and the step from eleven to eleven thousand was easily and quickly taken. By 850 Wandalbert of Prum had mounted them halfway. By the close of the century they had reached the eleven thousand, at which figure they remained. By that time also the vague story of their adventures showed definite color and outline. It was told over and over again, the varying details leading up always to the same sorrowful and glorious end.

Saint Ursula, the daughter of Theonotus, a dateless Christian king of Brittany, was sought in marriage by Prince Conon, son of a pagan king of Britain. Sometimes the situation is reversed. Theonotus is King of Britain, and Conon Prince of Brittany. But this is an unusual variant. As a rule, stress is laid upon the higher civilization of the continent, the comparative rudeness of the island. No British princess could have been described, as an old chronicler describes Saint Ursula, in terms that would have fitted a devout Christian Hypatia:

"She was not only graceful and beautiful, but of rare scholarship. Her mind was stored with knowledge and enlightened by wisdom. She knew the courses of the stars and of the winds; she was acquainted with the history of the world; she had read the poets and the philosophers. Above all she was versed in scholastic divinity, so that the doctors of the Church were amazed by her learning."

This accomplished lady was reluctant to marry. She sought excuses for delay, and was visited opportunely in a dream by an angel who bade her summon eleven thousand virgins, and go with them on a pilgrimage to Rome before consenting to the nuptials. Undismayed, she promised obedience, and set about fulfilling the conditions. The maidens, "spotless and noble," were collected, and the fleet set sail for Italy. Adverse winds, or perhaps ignorance on the part of the ladies—who, we are told, manned the sails—drove them northward. The pilgrims landed at Cologne, went to Basle, and thence made their way over the Alps to Rome. They were accompanied by angels who cleared roads through the snowdrifts, threw bridges over torrents, and at night pitched tents to shelter them. Thus guided and protected they reached the holy city, "a fair and wondrous host," and were honorably received by the Pope, Saint Cyriacus.

Here the undaunted Prince Conon joined them, and was baptized. On their way home they stopped, or were stopped, at Cologne, and were there barbarously murdered by the heathen Huns.

Now what has made this legendary princess more real to us than many a saint whose name is duly placed on the Roman Calendar, and duly chanted in the great Litany? Certainly not the heap of bones which the sacristan of St. Ursula's Church shows with an indulgent smile to skeptical tourists. No, it has been left for art to take the story under its august protection, to clothe it with beauty, to trick it out with every device that can win and hold attention. Carpaccio was in his splendid prime when he painted for the Scuola di San Orsola (a home for poor little Venetian girls) the series of pictures which now adorn the walls of the Accademia. Venice, like Florence, gave the best she could command to her orphaned children. The paintings tell in order every detail of the saint's story, from the coming of the British envoys to ask her hand down to her final martyrdom on the banks of the Rhine. The most beautiful of all is the well-known Dream, familiar to thousands who know little else about the amazing pilgrimage. Ursula lies sleeping in a vast, low Italian bed. Her crown, her slippers, and her little lap-dog are neatly disposed at its foot. The angel who enters the room, casting a radiance before him, is fair haired and of a gentle appearance. He looks as if he had come to bless the sleeper, and not to command a magnificent impossibility.

Rivaling the Dream is the lovely canvas which shows us Pope Cyriacus receiving the virgin and her train in Rome. It is a picture full of color and animation. Banners stream in the air, the rich vestments of the ecclesiastics glisten in the sunshine, the Castle of St. Angelo rises superbly in the background. This is the painting beloved by Gautier, who never could make up his mind whether he most deeply admired the princess with her adorable naïveté, her air of angelic coquetry, or the young prince, proud, charming, fiery, and seductive.

Carpaccio was not alone in his ardor for Saint Ursula, nor was Italy the only land that strove to do her honor. Tourists who are happy enough to go to Bruges, and wise enough to stay there instead of departing post-haste to the good food and pretty shops of Brussels, find their reward in strolling day after day to the Hospital of St.

John, and looking again and again and yet again
at Memling's masterpiece, La Châsse de Sainte
Ursule. There it stands, the most exquisite toy
(if one may without irreverence call a reliquary
a toy) in the world. Every inch of the miniature
Gothic chapel is covered with rich and lovely
work. On its sides are painted six scenes from
the virgin martyr's story. She goes with her
maidens to Cologne, to Basle, to Rome, where
the Pope awaits her, and where the British neo-
phytes are baptized. She returns to Cologne,
and the last panel shows her passively awaiting
death at the hands of a young Hun who bends his
bow with cautious deliberation. On one medallion
we see the apotheosis of the saint, and on the
other she shelters under her cloak the young
girls whose blessed patroness she has become.

To those who have fallen deeply in love with
this perfect example of Flemish art the Châsse
becomes a possession and a memory. To see it
one day is to desire inordinately to see it the
next; to bid it farewell is to carry away its
image in our hearts, and to think of it with secret
pleasure at strange hours and in unlovely places.
No other masters have done so well by Saint
Ursula as have Carpaccio and Memling; but
Palma Vecchio painted her, and so did Cima da

Conegliano, and Lorenzo di Credi, and Simoni di Martini. She stands as an altarpiece in the Cathedral of Cologne, and she adorns most exquisitely the famous Hours of Anne of Brittany. Two old and charming pictures in the Hôtel de Cluny tell the tale of her wanderings and of her martyrdom. A faded canvas in the museum of Seville represents her receiving with apathetic unconcern the stroke of a Hunnish swordsman, while the foreground is strewn with the neatly severed and bloodless heads of her companions. There was even a German painter whose name has been forgotten, but who was long known as the "Master of the Legend of Saint Ursula." Eighteen pictures illustrating her story came from his hand, and enriched the Church of St. Severin in Cologne. In St. Ursula's Church there is a recumbent figure of the virgin martyr, beautifully carved in alabaster, with a dove nestling at her feet; and also a series of small paintings which tell with an ingenious wealth of anachronisms the history of her high adventure. These paintings have been admirably reproduced, and were printed in color with an accompanying text in London, 1869.

Poets have not been unmindful of Saint Ursula, though she has never been to them the inspiration that she has been to painters. There is a metrical version of her legend, written in the latter half of the Fifteenth Century by Edmund Hatfield, a monk of Rochester. It is dedicated to Lady Margaret Beaufort, the mother of Henry the Seventh, and was one of the earliest works issued from the press of Wynkyn de Worde. Hatfield, like a good Englishman, claims all the personages of the story as British born. Theonotus—he spells the name Dyonothus—is in his poem a Christian king of Cornwall, and Conon is the son of Agrippinus, a pagan king of the Picts. Perhaps eleven thousand virgins seemed to him an incredible number for the Cornish coast to yield, for he urbanely explains that many of these Christian maids were in reality pagan matrons of irreproachable virtue who joined the expedition because of Ursula's great renown, and who were duly baptized in Rome. He gives the names of some of these ladies, and is loud in his praise of all.

Hatfield's narrative follows in leisurely fashion the familiar episodes of the story down to the massacre at Cologne. Ursula is the last to die, having scornfully rejected the advances of the Hunnish leader who seeks her hand:

This virtuous virgin abhorred his flesshely proffre,
In hym rebukynge with wordes mylde and sage;
The seed of Sathan her sappience might not suffre,
But grenned for woo with rancour he began to rage.
He drewe an arrowe his anger to assuage,
And perced the prudent prymerose thrughe ye brayne,
Commendynge her soule to Cryste with all courage;
Thus were these sayntes dysperpled, spoyled and slayne.

Heaven forbid that I should seek to rob a saint of one of the cardinal virtues; but "prudent prymerose" seems an ill-fitting epithet for Ursula. She was certainly prudent to refuse to marry the Hun; but she would have been more prudent still to have kept out of his way. Hers was the splendid spirit of enthusiasm, the courage, the confidence, the persuasive power which bends the will of man, wins the service of angels, and meets death with intrepidity.

There is a sombre old French song which asks the prayers of Saint Ursula for innocent girls before whom life lies darkly, as well as for the souls of the foul heathen who slew her in a cruel and alien land. Here and there we find her name in snatches of verse; and she has a place in the supremely modern poem of Remy de Gourmont, "Les Saintes de Paradis," with its rapturous imagery and its eminently non-liturgical invocations:

Agatha, stone and iron, Agatha, gold and silver,
Saint Agatha put fire in our blood.

Jeanne who resembles a wrathful angel,
Jeanne d'Arc put anger in our hearts.

Ursula carried away on the wings of a white bird,
Saint Ursula take our souls to the snows.

Nowhere have I been able to discover where
De Gourmont found his white bird. A dove,
symbol of innocence, occasionally accompanies
Saint Ursula; but no dove could carry her far
away. Her only emblem is the arrow which slew
her, and which was for her the key of Paradise.
There is, however, a very old German legend
which says that one of the eleven thousand virgins, "a holy maiden named Kovdula," escaped
the slaughter; and, fleeing to the shores of the
Rhine, beheld in a vision the souls of her companions, "a flock of doves, beating with their
white wings against the golden gates of Heaven."

Once established in the popular—and pious
—mind as patroness of young girls, the cult of
Saint Ursula spread rapidly over Europe. The
Sixteenth Century saw it at its height; and when
a well-born and far-seeing lady of Lombardy
conceived the design of founding a religious order for the education of little maids, it was but
natural that she should place it under the blessed

martyr's protection. Angela de Merici, subsequently canonized as Saint Angela, was born in Desenzano, a tiny town on Lake Garda. Early orphaned, and adopted by a wealthy uncle, she was generously educated and wisely counseled. There was not a great deal to be taught four hundred years ago (quality rather than quantity set the standard); but it is to the credit of Angela's imagination, no less than to the credit of her intelligence, that she proposed to teach girls in the systematic and orderly fashion common to the monastic schools for boys. If this instruction was to be more than a brief and perishable experiment, it must be entrusted to an order of nuns who would carry on to other generations the principles of their foundress. In her efforts to bridge the gap between the scholarship of the few and the contented ignorance of the many, this devout feminist appears very modern. It would almost seem as though the cherished idol of our day, literacy, had appealed to her robust intelligence.

There were difficulties to be encountered and overcome. Lombardy evinced no zeal for the education of its daughters, and the Church was wisely reluctant to recognize new religious orders. They sprang up like nettles, and would have choked her path if she had not weeded well. Angela strove for seventeen years to carry out her purpose, and the eighteenth year saw the little school established at Brescia, under the care of twelve women who received ecclesiastical sanction and were permitted to wear a habit, but who were never recognized as nuns. It was not until 1572, years after the death of their foundress, that the Ursulines received, through the patronage of Saint Charles Borromeo, the status of a monastic order. The Cardinal Archbishop of Milan, at all times as acute as he was holy, desired their presence in his city "to direct schools for little girls." He therefore obtained from Pope Gregory the Thirteenth a decree authorizing them to live in community, to take perpetual vows, and to create new foundations. The desire of Angela de Merici's heart was realized after that heart had been stilled, and the survival of her life's work was assured.

It is the lamentable habit of hagiographers to exclude from their narratives any circumstance which might possibly link them with life, to deny to the subjects of their pious memoirs any characteristic which savors too strongly of humanity. In their desire to be edifying they cease to be convincing. That the saint was pri-

marily a man or a woman with habits, and idio-
syncrasies, and purposes, and prejudices, is a
truth which they begin by ignoring as far as
possible, and end by forgetting altogether. What
they present for our consideration is a shining
assortment of virtues, but not a fellow creature
recognizable as such at any point of contact.

Now the foundress of the Ursulines was a very
holy woman; but she was also a pioneer. She essayed to do something that had not been done
before, which proves her to have been moved,
like Saint Ursula, by the spirit of adventure.
Saint Charles Borromeo, being himself en route
for canonization, honored no doubt her holiness;
but what he wanted was schools for girl children,
schools which should be intelligently conducted,
and have the quality of permanence. That he
thought well of the system of instruction which
Angela had carefully outlined is shown by his
counseling the nuns whom he established at
Milan to adhere to it as closely as possible:
"Follow the footsteps of your sisters in Brescia,"
he said. "There did your venerable mother plant
the tree which has borne good fruit." He also
ventured to assert that convent schools would
spread over all the Christian world: a prophecy
which has been amply fulfilled.

If textbooks were few and lessons were simple in the Sixteenth Century, the Brescian rules laid down for the guidance of teachers were models of common sense. The habit adopted by the community must be plain but of good texture so that it need not be often renewed. The members were permitted to walk the streets, but forbidden to loiter by the way. They must keep the fast days of the Church, but practise no additional austerities without the permission of director and superior. They must hear Mass and pray, but not linger in church when there is work to be done outside. They must unite the self-respect which they owe to themselves with the civility which they owe to their neighbors, and the patient kindness which is due to children. When given an order, or asked a favor, they must comply with a good grace, doing a thing as if they liked to do it.

The Ursulines were not general-utility nuns. Their purpose was to teach, and they were trained for no other work. But four years after they had been established in Milan there came to the doomed city the most terrible visitation of the plague that Italy had ever known. The part played by the cardinal archbishop in those awful days is now a page of history; but his

humble adjutants in the field have been less
highly honored. All we know is that when those
days were past, the survivors in the Ursuline
convent, few in numbers, haggard, spent, and
sad, received from Pope Gregory a blessing, and
a word of commendation for their valorous
services.

In 1596 the order was established in France
by Françoise de Bermond, canonized later by
Pius the Seventh. She appears to have been a
capable and humorous woman, whose recorded
maxims have a trenchant quality suggestive of
that model of all nuns, Saint Theresa. The great
Carmelite, who detested wordy arguments about
trifles, would have relished Françoise's counsel
to her novices: "If you have any opinion on a
subject under discussion, state it, give your reasons clearly and modestly, and then stop!"
Advice which, if followed, must have made the
convent recreation hour a pleasurable experience.

It is said that when the Ursulines came under
the favorable notice of Pope Paul the Third,
and he bestowed on them his formal approbation,
he observed to Saint Ignatius Loyola, "I am
giving you sisters." The Jesuits have always
been well affected to the order, a circumstance

which accounts for the summons to Quebec in
1639. Père Coton, the Jesuit confessor of Henry
the Fourth, was a firm friend. The Queen, Marie
de Medicis, frequently visited the famous convent in Paris, founded by Mme. de Sainte Beuve;
and there the little Dauphin was brought to recite his catechism to the nuns, and to play at
ball in the spacious gardens. This was the first
house to be strictly cloistered. The enclosure was
effected with solemn ceremonies on the 25th of
September, 1612. Cardinal de Retz, Archbishop
of Paris, locked the convent door, and gave the
key to the superior, while the imprisoned nuns
joyously intoned the *Te Deum*.

There is no need to dwell upon the part which
the teaching orders have played in France. For
centuries French women have been what French
convents have made them; and other nuns have
assumed a more important rôle than the Ursulines in the training of these capable, understanding, and dominant wives and mothers, who seldom mistake the shadow for the substance, and
who are content to bear the burden inseparable
from ascendency. The noteworthy characteristic
of Ursula's daughters is their valorous spirit. It
carried them as far afield as it had carried the
saint—to the snows of Quebec, and to the winter

roses of New Orleans. In the Reign of Terror it brought twenty-seven of them—a goodly number—to the finality of the guillotine. They played true to form when the Revolution tested the courage of its antagonists. It is said that the populace of Avignon, where part of the twenty-seven met their deaths, evinced a not unnatural irritation at the alacrity with which these "pious hypocrites" prepared to die; and of those who were guillotined at Valenciennes it was remarked: "They did not walk to the scaffold, they flew." A solitary nun, Angela Lepont, escaped for some unknown reason the fate of her companions. She lost her chance to suffer for Church and King; but she survived to reëstablish the community at Valenciennes, and to see little schoolgirls coming and going as sedately as though no whirlwind had swept France clean of all that was best and worst. Perhaps, when the work of reconstruction was heavy on her hands, and ineffaceable memories saddened her heart, she dreamed, like the maid Kovdula, of her happier companions winging their flight to Heaven:

The old road to Paradise is a crowded way.

Chapter II

MARIE GUYARD

THE city of Tours was, at the close of the Six-teenth Century, a singularly felicitous birth-place. Lying in the noble curve of the Loire, with a buried Roman town beneath its gray walls, and the mild skies of Touraine overhead, it was at once stirring and sedate. Enriched by the Church for seven hundred years, and by mer-chants and craftsmen for two hundred years, it lacked neither the activities of wealth nor the traditions of ecclesiastical culture. The Tour de l'Horloge and the Tour Charlemagne (built over the tomb of his wife, Luitgarde) defended its whole area. The great abbey church of St. Martin had survived age and ill-usage. The shrine of the saint, despoiled but not desecrated, was visited by pious pilgrims. The Cathedral of St. Gatianus, begun in 1170, had been completed for fifty years—a charming if not a lordly church, with good stained glass and a beautiful choir. Artists and architects, goldsmiths, glass workers, and silk weavers thronged to Tours, bringing with them the luxuries and amenities of life.

The pride of the city centered in the painter, Jean Fouquet, and in the sculptor, Michel Colomb, who made the lovely effigies of the royal children, offspring of Charles the Eighth and Anne of Brittany, and placed at their heads and feet small devout angels, the most adorable little guardians in the world.

In this ancient and historic city, under these favoring skies, Marie Guyard was born on the 18th of October, 1599. Her father, Florent Guyard, was a silk merchant of plain extraction; her mother, a serene and intelligent woman, was a descendant of the illustrious house of Barbon de la Bourdaisière. They appear to have enjoyed that modest competency to which French thrift has always given dignity and ease. Of Marie's childhood little is recorded save that she loved fanciful and imaginative play (children's imaginations were not then starved out by a surfeit of mechanical toys), and that she was a pitiful little girl to beggars, of whom there have been plenty in Tours since the days of Saint Martin.

Père François Xavier de Charlevoix, the earliest and best of Marie Guyard's biographers, prefaces his work with a lengthy introduction in which he admits that his task has been a diffi-

cult one because the great Ursuline was confessedly a mystic, and mysticism was to the
Eighteenth Century (Charlevoix's volume was
published in 1724) a delusion and a snare. We
are more receptive to-day because more familiar
with scholastic philosophy which offers an avenue
of approach. William Penn was a mystic, and
so was Jeanne d'Arc, and Saint Catherine of
Siena, and that capable woman, Saint Theresa.
All experienced their first revelations at an early
age. Penn was eleven when the celestial light
flooded his chamber, and the celestial whisper
stirred his soul. Catherine was six when she saw
the vision of the Christ Child, clad in pontifical
vestments and with a shining mitre on his head,
which is the way a baby girl, familiar with Italian
churches, would naturally conceive of Him. Marie
Guyard was seven when the image of the Re-
deemer smiled at her from the opening heavens.
Jeanne d'Arc was thirteen when the impelling
voices first summoned her to action. These spiritual manifestations made Jeanne a soldier, and
Penn a pacifist, and Catherine a sublimated poli-
tician, and Marie a pioneer. So it is that *les
âmes bien nées* correspond unerringly with grace,
and fulfill their destinies.

Never too easily, indeed. When Marie Guyard was fourteen she greatly desired to enter the Convent of St. Benoit, at Beaumont, where Mme. de la Bourdaisière, a relative of her mother, was superior. Her youth made this impossible; and three years later her parents received an eligible offer for her hand, which they promptly accepted, communicating the circumstance to their daughter in the decisive fashion common to that day. The suitor was M. Martin, a wealthy manufacturer of silk. He probably had —all Frenchmen do have—half-a-dozen Christian names; but not one of them is mentioned in the few casual paragraphs vouchsafed him by Marie's biographers. All that we are told is that she married him when she was seventeen, and that "an air of enjoyment," inseparable from her years, made her seem a happy bride.

She was certainly a busy wife. Martin, as was then the custom, housed and fed his principal employees. Marie's hands were full of work, her mind was full of care. Much that she needed to know in later years as the head of a convent and a school, she learned in her husband's establishment. Charlevoix says that the artisans showed her "a filial tenderness and confidence"—which is a curious way of phrasing their affection, in view of her extreme youth. The domestic servants were many, and she ruled them with good-humored vigilance. The model wife of Proverbs could not well have surpassed her in diligence and discretion. Her spouse seems to have been affectionately disposed, and fully alive to her merits. The birth of a son so filled his heart with content that there was nothing left for him but to die, which he accordingly did, after two years of married life.

It is impossible not to feel a certain sympathy for M. Martin. He was admittedly a kind husband, and an eminently respectable man. He must have had aims, and purposes, and high hopes of what life might bring him. At the very least he had his own individuality, his own place in this world and in the next. Yet he is always alluded to as a mere episode in his wife's history, and, from the point of view of her biographers, a stumbling-block in her career. Abbé Casgrain even hints at some deep-rooted sorrow in her heart, inseparable from her married life. If this sorrow existed, the cause is not far to seek. It was, after all, not the life she had desired; and while it was good of its kind, it was not supremely good for her. Such truths are never plainly spoken in pious narratives; but we always discern a sense of relief when superfluous husbands and wives are removed from the scene of action.

Be this as it may, Marie Guyard Martin was a widow at nineteen, in good repute, comely to look upon, and with as many suitors as Penelope. Her mother-in-law, to whom had fallen the direction of the business, greatly desired her capable assistance; but in a few months old Mme. Martin followed her son to the grave, and Marie was left free from all ties save that of motherhood. For some reason, never sufficiently explained, she who should have been rich was poor. There are vague allusions to a lawsuit which she appears to have lost; but Charlevoix and Casgrain are so taken up with telling us how nobly she bore reverses that they have little to say as to why she had reverses to bear. They are seemingly acquainted with every sentiment of her soul, every pious thought and word and prayer; but they fail to make clear to us why the widow and son of a well-to-do manufacturer should have been despoiled of their inheritance.

She was not too poor to lack applicants for her hand, and those who thought they had her welfare most at heart advocated a second marriage as a natural and seemly solution of her life's problems. But Marie no longer owed obedience to anyone. She had attained freedom, and the privilege of deciding for herself what she had better do. What she wanted to do was only too clear to her understanding. The desire of her womanhood, like the desire of her childhood, was to enter a convent. Her spiritual nature sought this outlet for its emotions; her human nature was deeply attuned to solitude, silence, and an orderly mode of existence, a soothing and systematic routine.

But there was her baby boy. Marie's wisdom was never more manifest than in the two decisions she made at this crucial period, and from which she never swerved. While her son was yet a child he needed above all things a mother's care, and her plain duty was to keep him by her side, and train him as best she could. After he was twelve, he would need the guardianship of men. She would then relax her hold, and commit his education to a religious order, the Jesuits, or the Benedictines. The Seventeenth Century, unlike the Twentieth, did not regard a youth as the personal property of his mother. That he should, or could, be taught by women was foreign to their way of thought. They had a well-grounded conviction that only men could fit a boy for manhood.

An older sister of Marie's, Anne Guyard, had
also married a wealthy citizen of Tours, and he
opened his doors to his sister-in-law, being a far-
sighted man who knew the advantage of having
under his roof such a supremely capable young
woman. He was an officer in the artillery, charged
with the transporting of military supplies from
one province to another. His income was ample,
his household large, his duties called him repeatedly from home. Marie began by being his
housekeeper, and ended by taking his multitu-
dinous affairs under her personal supervision.
His kitchen, his stables, his office—she managed them all; yet found time for hours of prayer,
and for the importunities of the poor. Her son,
who has written a few intimate recollections of
his mother at this period of her life, tells us three
things that are striking and illustrative. The first
is that she was never flustered, and consequently
never annoyed, by inconsequent demands upon
her attention. The second, that she dearly loved
to be alone when such an indulgence was possible. The third, that she was unvaryingly gentle
and consolatory in her attentions to the poor:
"She approached them with respect as living
representatives of Christ." This is a wonderful
sentence. The shocking thing about poverty is

the contempt it engenders in the hearts of the rich. The more active and efficient their measures of relief, the deeper is this unconscious or half-conscious scorn, which is accepted unprotestingly by the objects of their charity; but which must, nevertheless, be the most unpalatable drop in their cup of bitterness. Only a profoundly spiritual nature can daily contemplate their natural incapacity, their imperfect equipment, and their many mischances, yet bear always in mind one brief decisive sentence of Holy Writ: "Inasmuch as ye have done it unto one of the least of these my brethren, ye have done it unto me."

So the years slipped by over Marie's head. They were not happy years. If she could not find happiness in superintending her own household, how should she expect to find it in superintending her brother-in-law's? Yet her life held many consolations. She was busy and efficient. She was devout and composed. Her son grew to vigorous boyhood by her side. Her surroundings were beautiful. Citizens of Tours grew familiar with the sedate figure of the young widow as she walked the pleasant streets, or knelt in the vast old Church of St. Julian, or held up the little Claude to see the marble children of Colomb, or strolled through the cloisters of the Petit St. Martin, now so pitifully wrecked, but then complete and lovely. Outside the city's gates stood the noble and partly preserved Abbey of Marmoutier. There Saint Gatianus and Saint Martin, who between them Christianized Tours, retired from time to time to live like hermits in rocky caves (Marie must have sincerely envied them this blessed privilege); there Charles Martel defeated the Saracens in 720; and there the seven sleepers, like those of Ephesus, lay awaiting the hour which should summon them to give testimony of their faith.

When Marie was thirty and her son was twelve she felt herself free to fulfill her heart's desire and enter a convent. As the day of her deliverance drew near, this desire augmented in intensity. She had always loved solitude, and she had spent her adult years in close and complicated contact with her fellow creatures. She had always coveted the serenity of obedience, and it had been her task to control and direct the unruly:

> Her life was turning, turning,
>   In mazes of heat and sound,
> But for peace her soul was yearning——

and now at last it stood close at her doors—the peace that passeth all understanding. Her choice of an order was determined by circumstance. The Ursulines had recently established themselves in Tours, and she had come under the notice of their superior, Mère Françoise de Saint Bernard. This highly intelligent nun offered to receive her without a dower, being as well aware as Saint Theresa that, while a wealthy novice is always a welcome addition to a convent, a woman of character, capacity, and holiness is a veritable godsend.

It was natural that Marie's sister and brother-in-law should have been unwilling to lose her services; and it was equally natural that as they could not well plead their own convenience as a sufficient reason for keeping her in the world, they should have advanced the stronger argument of her duty to her son. This was a matter which she had well considered, and of which she had never lost sight in the years of her widowhood. She had striven always to wean the child from a too dependent affection for her. The grave gentleness of her manner toward him was unbroken by words or acts of tenderness. She never kissed or fondled him, or encouraged him to offer her any childish caress. There was un-doubted affection on her part and on his; but it was denied a natural outlet, and this denial was meant to lessen the pain of an approaching separation. Marie watched over her son with wise solicitude, and he reposed in her the implicit confidence which a child gives to a parent whom he has never detected in deception or injustice.

It is hard for us to-day to regard with sym-pathy and understanding a situation which was in accord with its own time and place. Every man disapproves of what he does not do, and every generation disapproves of preceding gen-erations for much the same reason. Dr. Johnson expressed this point of view with admirable pre-cision when he said of Christians outside the English Establishment: "In everything in which they differ from us, they are wrong." The over-whelming sentimentalism of our day, the soft-ness of our moral fibre, are at variance with what Baron von Hügel calls the "astringency of re-ligion": a quality which dominated the years of persecution and the years of contest, which sac-rificed much that was amiable in personal con-tacts, but which made for fearlessness and fortitude. "I hold," wrote Von Hügel, "this astringent emotion, this asceticism, this apparent hardness, this combat and concentration, to be, in the right place and proportion, an absolutely essential constituent of the Christian outlook. Where this element is not, there is not authentic Christianity, but some sentimental humanitarianism, or other weakening inadequacy."

Weakening inadequacy formed no part of Marie Guyard's mental or spiritual make-up. She was sure that her call to a cloistered life came from God. That it fitted her own disposition and desires was not, in her eyes, a reason for renouncing it. She considered sensibly that she was more likely to be of service in a community if she were happy under its rule. Her son appears to have been a perfectly normal boy. Not a single instance of precocious piety on his part has been told us, so we may be sure that there was none to tell. On the other hand, the adventurous spirit common to boyhood drew him now and then into trouble. On one occasion he left his uncle's house to walk to Paris, of whose whereabouts he knew nothing, but of whose wonders he had heard much. Happily, three days' wandering carried him no farther than to Blois, where a friend of the family found him, hungry, tired, and temporarily convinced that home and school and bed and dinner were better for little boys than freedom and the unfriendly world.

To this lad, when he was twelve, Marie communicated her resolve to enter the convent of the Ursulines, and gravely asked him to authorize her withdrawal from the world. The boy, called on for the first time to give permission where he had always sought it, put several anxious questions. Was she going far away? Would he never see her again? Being told that she would remain in Tours, and that he might see her daily, he said with a gravity equal to her own: "Then you have my consent." In his account of this singular interview, Dom Claude Martin, who had become a Benedictine monk, comments upon his mother's self-repression. "It seemed the time and the place," he writes simply, "for some mark of affection. But even then she did not offer to kiss me. She blessed me, and made the sign of the cross on my forehead, and that was all."

On the 25th of January, 1631, Marie Guyard entered the Ursuline convent in Tours. It was the feast of the conversion of Saint Paul. Her father and mother, her sisters, her brother-in-law (quiescent but unreconciled), and her son accompanied her to the door. Within, Mère

Françoise stood waiting to receive her into the novitiate. The goal, so long desired, was won at last. Behind her the past lay like a troubled dream. Before her the future, wilder than any dream, was veiled in comforting obscurity.

Chapter III

THE CALL

THE life of a novice who enters a convent at thirty-two is an incongruous one, which only tact and resolute endeavor can make normal. Marie, a widow, a mother, a woman of affairs and of wide experience, was singularly out of place amid the light-hearted, light-headed young girls who had yet to be instructed in all the duties of their profession. Wisely and humbly she did her best to render herself acceptable to them. When they talked, she was content to listen. When they advised her, she accepted and followed their counsel. In the words of Charlevoix, "she endeavored to hide from them her superior accomplishments, and was content if they did not find her insipid."

Of her supreme happiness there is no shadow of doubt. Her nature fulfilled itself in this suave and regulated life, in the order and quiet, in the opportunities to obey, in the rapture of meditation and the profound peace of prayer. The convent seemed to her a veritable paradise, a heaven-sent refuge from the tormenting cares of the world. She confesses that when she walked through the cloisters she seemed to tread on air, so light was her heart, so welcome were the protecting walls. "When my eyes fell upon my religious habit I would raise my hand and gently touch my veil, to make sure that I really and truly possessed the joy of living in the house of God, and that I belonged to Him." Like all mystics she was sometimes happy in prayer, and sometimes unduly sad; but from first to last she never doubted the felicity of a cloistered life. She summed up the situation in a few bliss-laden words: *"Ah, que c'est un grand répos à une âme religieuse!"*

One definite advantage accrued to this devout soul from monastic discipline: it put an end to her excessive asceticism. So long as she was free, Marie Guyard had yielded more and more to that passion for self-denial, for self-inflicted hardships, which may lead to sanctity or to madness. She wore a hair shirt, she slept on boards, she fasted with cruel rigor. Now such acts of mortification were forbidden unless practised in common with her companions, and according to rule. Mère Françoise de Saint Bernard explained to the new novice that she had a duty to her neighbor as well as to God. The Ursulines were not a meditative order, they taught, and teaching required bodily health and a nicely preserved mental balance. So far, Marie's youth and vigor had carried her triumphantly through the sufferings she inflicted upon herself as well as through the annoyances inflicted upon her by others; but now youth had fled. Thirty-two was an age which called for prudence and the conservation of force. Moreover, as the superior well knew, asceticism is infectious. A convent of nuns outdoing one another in penitential exercises would be as intractable and inadequate as a convent of nuns shirking the prescribed fasts and vigils. The cardinal virtue of temperance, inherited by Christianity from paganism, is essential to communal well-being.

When, after a year's novitiate, Marie was permitted to take her vows, to become a full-fledged nun, and to receive her official title, Mère Marie de l'Incarnation, she was at once appointed mistress of the novices among whom she had so recently lived. It was a post for which she was eminently well fitted. Order and system were inseparable from her being. A sympathetic understanding made her a wise and kind directress. Her superior intelligence enabled her to teach. The young nuns regarded her with ad-

miration which might have mounted to unreason-
ing enthusiasm had she been less aloof, less grave
in manner, less direct in speech. She wrote for
their benefit a series of instructions which were
subsequently published under the title of *L'École
Sainte*. They are couched in graceful and supple
French, with a choice of words, deliberate or
unconscious, which now and then convey a sudden and flashing picture to the mind. Père Charlevoix, who was himself a writer of uncommon
animation, says of them: "The truths of religion could not be defined with more clearness,
precision and simplicity."

As the quiet months lengthened into years the
life of Mère Marie flowed on in an even current,
and it seemed as though the French convent
would witness the flowering and the fading of
her powers. The murmur of the outside world
came muffled to her ears, the agitations of the
worldly served only to accentuate the unruffled
calm of her systematized existence. The young
Claude had been placed at the Jesuit school in
Rennes. He seems to have inherited a fair share
of his mother's intelligence, but very little of her
sobriety. He was a good student, but a born
rover. Just as he had wandered away from Tours
as a child, so he wandered back to it as a boy,

making his unsolicited appearance at his aunt's door, and trusting to her affection for a welcome. As Rennes would have no more of him, he was sent, under the care of a very able priest, Père de la Haye, to the school at Orléans. There he consented to remain, and there he plodded along the paths of learning until he had completed his course of philosophy.

Then came the summons which was to change Marie's placid life into one of adventure and hardship, which was to turn the secluded nun, known only to the little city of Tours, into a pioneer whose name is a familiar and cherished one in the land of her adoption, and in the annals of her order. The first clear and persuasive words were written by Père Le Jeune, the superior of the Jesuit missions in New France, and by far the liveliest chronicler their ranks could boast. Of all the letters and reports published in those remarkable records, the Jesuit *Relations*, none can rival his in vicacity and charm. He had lived a hard and half-savage life among the Indians, and he had helped materially to build up the comparative civilization of Quebec. Now, having seen the completion of the first hospital, he asked for a school and orphanage. The boys were taught by the priests; but there was no one to instruct the little French girls, or Christianize the little Indians. Money was needed for this purpose, money and nuns. France had both in plenty. What would she spare to her colony?

His words met with an immediate response. There was living then in Alençon a young widow, wealthy, well-born, generous, and devout, whose life had been vastly different from Marie Guyard's, and whose temperament contrasted sharply with the disciplined restraint of the Ursuline. Marie Madeleine de Chauvigny was the only child of the Seigneur de Vaubougon, a gentleman whose fortune equalled his birth, and whose virtues—so Abbé Casgrain assures us—surpassed both. Virtuous he no doubt was; but as a father he seems to have been a happy combination of Squire Western and the choleric Lord Capulet. The young Marie was brilliantly educated, according to the standards of her day. Her biographers unite in saying that she desired all her life to become a nun. They seem to think that this assertion is necessary to justify her existence. But she never did become a nun, and there is no evidence that she ever wanted to. She seems to have coveted independence as keenly as Marie Guyard coveted subjection.

It is true that when Mlle. de Chauvigny was seventeen she went to make a religious retreat in a neighboring convent, this being a common practice among Catholic girls and women. It is true also that she went without her father's permission, being probably aware that he would not have given it, and seeking to escape a parental rebuff. In this, however, she had reckoned without the parental temper. It took M. de Chauvigny but a few hours to follow his daughter to the convent, pack her into the waiting carriage, and convey her swiftly home. The next morning he informed her that he had chosen for her husband a young man whom he deeply esteemed, Charles de Grivel de la Peltrie, a wealthy landowner, and a cadet of the noble house of Tounois. It was in every respect a desirable alliance, even for his only child and future heiress, and he trusted that she would be gratified by his choice.

Marie begged, as was but natural, for a little time in which to make up her mind; or, if that implied too great a liberty on her part, for a little time in which to grow accustomed to her future husband; but her father would hear of no delay. There was, he considered, no surer way of growing accustomed to a man than by marry-

ing him. He met her arguments and entreaties
by saying with Lord Capulet:

Get thee to church o' Thursday!

(or words to that effect); and within a few weeks
of her unwise visit to the convent, his daughter
was splendidly and very securely married.

M. de la Peltrie, like the humbler M. Martin,
proved to be an unexceptionable husband. Like
M. Martin, he was happy in his married life.
Like M. Martin, he discreetly died a few years
after marriage, leaving the path clear for his
wife's future activities. It was a trifle dangerous
to wed a woman who had an appointed destiny.
Mme. de la Peltrie's only child, a daughter, died
in infancy. In her early widowhood she read Père
Le Jeune's appeal for a school, for nuns to conduct it, and primarily for funds. Was there no
generous lady who would do for the children of
New France what the Duchesse d'Aiguillon had
so nobly done for the sick and hurt? It seemed
to her that here was work fitted to her hands.
She was young, strong, well educated, wealthy
in her own right, and the heiress of a still larger
fortune. She was ardent, enthusiastic, and adventurous. What better could she do with her

life than devote it to little Indians who needed
all that she could give?

Again she reckoned without her father who was
not, and who never meant to be, a negligible
factor in his family. He wanted his daughter
to marry again, to marry soon, and to marry
well. He wanted grandchildren of his own, and
he declined to accept as substitutes the little
heathens of Quebec. In the clearest possible
words he gave Mme. de la Peltrie to understand
that she should never leave France with his permission, and that if she left without it, she would
forfeit every penny of her inheritance.

It was a serious dilemma. In the Seventeenth
Century a French daughter, even a married
daughter, did not lightly defy her parents. Moreover, the estate of Vaubougon was essential to
the perfection of Mme. de la Peltrie's plans. She
understood the barriers in her way, and she took
refuge in that age-old sanctuary of bullied
women, deceit. The tale of this deceit is so
curious, and the accounts of it are so confusing,
that we can but follow the narratives as they
are given, and accept the most probable solution.

What we know is that there appeared on the
scene at this juncture a certain M. Jean Louvigny
de Bernières, or, as the name is sometimes given,

M. Jean de Bernières Louvigny, a man of position and influence who held the post of treasurer at Caen. Charlevoix represents him as a suitor of Mme. de la Peltrie's, and one so acceptable to her father that he assured his daughter he would die if she did not consent to the marriage. "This declaration," says the vivacious biographer, "which could not be taken literally, made little impression upon her." Abbé Casgrain affirms that the young widow herself chose M. de Bernières as an ally and accomplice, confiding to him her cherished plans, and asking him to go through the form of marriage with her, so that she could carry them out under the protection of his name. This he manfully refused to do; and it was only after many arguments and repeated solicitations that he could be brought so far as to make a formal offer for her hand. The delight with which this offer was received by M. de Chauvigny filled the reluctant suitor with fresh agitation; and it was then resolved that, as neither the gentleman nor the lady wanted to be married, they would merely pretend they had been, and so cozen the world at large—if such a thing were possible—and particularly the irascible Seigneur of Vaubougon.

This is one version of the story. Most com-

mentators take it for granted that M. de Bernières and Mme. de la Peltrie were married as
a matter of convenience, and with a mutual understanding of the somewhat complicated situation. What neither of them had foreseen was the
sudden death of M. de Chauvigny, whom they
had planned to circumvent, and who expired,
poor old gentleman, happy in the belief that he
had had his own way to the last. Neither had it
occurred to them that Mme. de la Peltrie's relatives would bring suit against her as incapable of
administering her estate, and ask that she should
be restrained from excessive expenditure. The
case was tried in Rouen, before the Parlement de
Normandie, and decided in the defendant's favor; the judges expressing their belief that money
spent on the needy was as well bestowed as money
hoarded for heirs.

Now at last the road seemed clear. Mme.
de la Peltrie was able and ready to finance the
long-desired school and orphanage in Quebec.
She went to Paris to consult the proper authorities, and there had the rare good fortune to meet
that noblest and sweetest of saints, Vincent de
Paul, and to confide to him her hopes and en-
deavors. There were still minor obstacles in her
way; but the lady possessed her full share of

that quality which in her father was called obstinacy, but which in her went by the kinder
name of determination. Her efforts were admirably seconded by M. de Bernières who had followed her to Paris. The choice of the Ursulines
as a teaching order was mainly due to Père Le
Jeune. It only remained to select from many
eager aspirants the nuns best fitted for such difficult and dangerous work.

All this time Mère Marie de l'Incarnation fulfilled her round of duties in the convent of Tours.
She knew (the sisterhood knew) that the Jesuits
in Quebec had asked for nuns to teach. She knew,
after the lapse of months, that efforts were being
made to supply their need. And deep down in her
secret heart she knew that this would be her appointed field of labor. In dreams she saw the
wild, wide wastes of snow, and heard the com-
pelling summons that had no need to couch itself in words. She never doubted the reality of
this call, and she never tried to break the bonds
which held her in her native town. She bent her
will into accord with God's will. She strove to
cleanse herself of any aspiration to go, save as
an instrument in God's hands. It was only by
complete detachment from desire that she could
make sure of a correspondence with God's grace.

In effect, the solidity of her merits threatened
her with defeat. M. d'Eschaux, the Archbishop
of Tours, had no desire to see his convent robbed
of its ablest nuns for the enrichment of New
France. He represented to Mme. de la Peltrie
that she would do better to draw her recruits
from the well-stocked house in Paris which
could furnish all she required. But the Seigneur
de Vaubougon's daughter knew her own mind,
and had her own way. She had heard from Père
Poncet de la Rivière, who was preparing to sail
for Quebec, of Mère Marie's acquirements, and
she would accept no unworthy substitute. The
convent of Tours was closed to the laity. She
actually wheedled the archbishop, whom she was
about to rob, into giving directions that she
should be received as though she were a nun.
In truth no abbess could have had a more im-
pressive welcome. Conducted ceremoniously into
the cloister chapel, she was given the episcopal
prie-Dieu on which to kneel, while the nuns sang
the *Veni Creator* and the *Te Deum*, and the convent bell pealed joyously. Afterwards she was
presented to the superior, and was embraced
by the choir sisters, every one of whom secretly
hoped that she might be chosen to accompany
the expedition.

Two only went, Mère Marie, and a young nun, Marie de Saint Bernard, a vigorous and spirited girl who could be trusted to bear hardships lightly. Conceiving that she owed her good fortune to the intercession of Saint Joseph, she asked and obtained permission to change her name to Marie de Saint Joseph, thus slighting one saint to compliment another. Her father, M. de la Troche, Seigneur de Savonnières et de Saint Germain, resolutely opposed her departure. So, for that matter, did Mère Marie's family, with less excuse, she being of mature years and a nun of long standing. Nevertheless they remained faithful to the good old tradition upon which all family life is built—opposition. They filled the air with their clamor, and vainly tried to persuade her son, then peacefully studying for the priesthood in Orléans, to add his protest to theirs.

M. de la Troche was of an irresolute disposition. When first informed that his daughter desired to go to Quebec, he refused to allow her to leave France. Then the solicitations of a pious Carmelite nun, a friend of his household, so wrought upon his feelings that he sent a letter of consent—a letter couched in language of such parental tenderness that when it was read aloud

in the Ursuline community, its hearers, so we
are told, melted into happy tears. It was too
soon for rejoicing. Members of M. de la Troche's
noble family, including the Bishop of La Rochelle, represented to him that he did wrong in
permitting his young daughter to cross the sea
to a savage land where she would probably encounter women of evil lives. This uncalled-for
suggestion (Quebec was a settlement of almost
monastic propriety) so distressed the tractable
old gentleman that he despatched a trusty mes-
senger to Paris—the travelers had gotten that
far on their journey—with instructions to conduct Mère Saint Joseph back to Tours without
fail and without delay. She did not go. Knowing her parent, she sent instead a letter so full
of submission, of pleading, and of reassurance,
that once more he yielded his consent to her departure. Before he had time to change his mind
again, she was on the ocean, and recall was impossible.

In Paris the nuns were lodged in the Ursuline
convent of the Faubourg St.-Jacques. The indefatigable M. de Bernières had arranged every
detail of their short journey, and attended to
every need. Mère Marie pronounces him in one
of her letters to be *"un homme ravissant,"* a

phrase of unusual warmth which is rapidly explained away by her heart-felt admiration for the capacity with which he conducted their affairs. Visitors of distinction thronged to see them. The Duchesse d'Aguillon, whose generosity had equipped Quebec with its Hôtel Dieu, and that very noble lady, the Comtesse de Brienne, carried them to St. Germain, where the Queen, Anne of Austria, desired their presence. She received them honorably, and with the liveliest curiosity, asking many questions about the voyage which they had not yet taken, about New France which they had never seen, and about the Indians concerning whom they knew as little as she did.

A third nun was added to the party in Paris. Also a young girl named Charlotte Barré, who was later received into the novitiate as Mère Catherine de Saint Ignace. There were the usual difficulties in securing a sailing from Dieppe. Vessels were few, freightage was heavy, accommodations were limited. Mme. de la Peltrie, impatient as ever of delay, proposed to charter a boat of her own. It was a small boat, and M. de Bernières considered that the voyage would be sufficiently uncomfortable on a bigger one. He counseled patience. The new nun was withdrawn, owing to the determined opposition of her family, and her place was filled by another whose relatives were either more compliant or less influential. M. de Bernières exerted himself incessantly on behalf of his charges. Mère Marie, more and more alive to his perfection, called him their guardian angel, and deplored the necessity of parting from so kind and useful a friend. It was proposed that he also should travel to Quebec, but this he firmly declined. Even a guardian angel may conceivably weary of his task.

There sailed then from Dieppe on the 4th of May, 1639, the three Ursulines, Mme. de la Peltrie and her young companion, three nursing nuns bound for the newly erected hospital in Quebec, and three Jesuit priests, Père Poncet de la Rivière, Père Chaumont, and Père Barthélemy Vimont, who had been made superior of the Canadian missions. The day was sparklingly clear. The sea lay blue and beautiful beneath a cloud-flecked sky. A fresh wind filled the sails. The voyagers looked their last upon the pleasant land of France which they were leaving forever. M. de Bernières went quietly back to his estate at Alençon. A great calm filled his soul.

Chapter IV

CHAMPLAIN

THE Quebec for which Mère Marie was bound in 1639 was vastly different from the Quebec which was to receive Père Marquette in 1666. Twenty-seven years sufficed to change the rude settlement into a civilized town, where life was safe, where comfort was the rule, and where pleasures were not altogether unknown. That was the Quebec to which the great Frontenac brought security and stability. Trade flourished, order reigned, and the officers of the garrison amused themselves and their friends by playing Corneille, like the talented and spirited young men they no doubt were. The Quebec of 1639 was the struggling colony which a greater man than Frontenac, Samuel de Champlain, had founded, nourished, lost, recovered, and loved until his dying day. Its story is the story of wild adventure, sober effort, and sustained gallantry. No page in history can better show the enduring quality of French courage, which failure makes persistent, and disaster quickens into flame.

What magnet drew Jacques Cartier three times over the sea before the fourth voyage (which is the first of which we have any record) brought him to the coast of Newfoundland, and the fifth to the mouth of the St. Lawrence? He was then a man over forty, the son and grandson of mariners. From his birthplace, St.-Malo, a proud city "virgin of English," he had seen countless ships sail into the sunset. The star of his destiny burned in the northern sky. He raised the first cross on the shore of Gaspé Bay, sang the first *Vexilla Regis*, and proffered the first trade to the natives of that inhospitable shore. He entered the St. Lawrence, wintered in Quebec (then an Indian village named Stadacoma), sailed up the river as far as the site of Montreal, and heard from the savages of inland seas, "where a man might travel on the face of the waters for many moons in the same direction."

This much knowledge was bought at a heavy price. Cartier lost so many men from cold and scurvy that he abandoned one of his ships, the timbers of which were uncovered from a mud-bank three hundred years later. Because he had no gold or copper to take back to France, he resolved in an evil hour to capture a few Indians, more especially Donnacoma, the headman of

the village, and carry them home as living wit-
nesses of his words.

It was a black deed, all too easily accomplished, and bringing nothing but trouble in its
wake. Life in France was as hard on the savages
as life in Canada had been hard on the French.
All save one little girl sickened and died; and
when, five years later, Cartier returned to Stadacoma, he found the once friendly Indians sullen
and hostile. This last expedition of 1541 had
been sponsored by the Sieur de Roberval, a
gentleman of Picardy, who aspired to plant a
colony on the banks of the St. Charles. The site
was well chosen, but the men were bad colonists.
Dissatisfied from the start, they proved themselves unequal to the hardships of their life, and
unfitted for the heroic task of self-dependence.
One thought possessed them, a desire to return
to France; and all who lived long enough did
so. This was Cartier's last voyage. He found
no backer for another, and he spent his remaining years pleasantly enough in writing an account of his adventures. The narrative made
good reading, but was not especially informative.
To this intrepid sailor an Indian was simply an
Indian. His language, save for a list of useful
words, was necessarily unknown. His tribe and

his traditions were matters of indifference. The maps, which undoubtedly accompanied the manuscript, have been lost. Cartier died in 1557. His statue stands in the Place de la Hollande, St.-Malo; and in the Hôtel de Ville there hangs an apocryphal portrait which looks as its painter conceived a master mariner ought to look— strong, bold, self-assured, and arrogant.

The latter half of the Sixteenth Century saw a lull in French schemes of colonization. Catholics and Huguenots were so hard at work fighting over their respective creeds that exhausted France had neither time nor money to spare to the New World. But the memory of Cartier's exploits never faded from his countrymen's minds, and the spirit of adventure which he had helped to fire embodied itself fifty years later in a figure of heroic proportions, one of the great pioneers of civilization, and a maker of history in the best sense of the word.

Samuel de Champlain was born in 1567 in the little port of Brouage, now surrounded by salt marshes. Sprung from a hardy and a roving line, he served as a soldier in the war of the League, and as a sailor on the Spanish Main. He had already attained the rank of royal geographer when he headed his first expedition to

Canada in 1603. This expedition was financed
by the Sieur de Chastes, a gentleman of the court,
and the commandant at Dieppe. Unfortunately
he died while his company was exploring the St.
Lawrence, and the trade monopoly he had enjoyed was transferred to the Sieur de Monts, a
Huguenot nobleman and the governor of Pons.
The new commissioner was bound to transport
to Canada one hundred colonists every year.
Merchants of St.-Malo, Honfleur, Rouen, and
Rochelle were keen to join in the adventure;
Champlain, who had returned to France, was
keener still to head it. Two boatloads of artisans
and agriculturists were fitted out, with a wise
old pilot, Pontgravé, to look after their safety,
and a Paris lawyer, Marc Lescarbot, to tell the
tale of their adventures.

The first settlement on an island in Passama-
quoddy Bay, which they named St. Croix, failed
signally for lack of fresh water and proper food.
De Monts returned to France in the autumn of
1605 for supplies; and his companions made a
home for themselves amid the snows of Acadia.
Here, according to Lescarbot, they led a hard,
but by no means disagreeable, life. Their annal-
ist was that *rara avis* in those days, a philosopher
as tolerant as Montaigne. Convinced that bigotry

was the most futile of human qualities, and that nothing would make men who thought at all think alike, he used to tell with glee how Charles the Fifth had learned tolerance from clock making. The emperor became an expert craftsman during the years of his retirement in the Monastery of St. Yuste; yet, in spite of his proficiency, his clocks never would strike in unison; and he fell to asking himself whether it were possible to force men's minds into accord, when he failed to accomplish this perfect precision with wheels and springs over which he had apparent control.

From Lescarbot we learn how Champlain, a leader of men as well as a maker of history, kept his party in good health and spirits during the long winter months. He organized his famous Ordre de Bon Temps, which regulated their days, smoothed over difficulties, saw to it that they were "cleanly and merry at food," and gave to every man a chance to entertain his neighbors. It was the experience of these two years in Acadia which filled him with confidence in his fellow countrymen, and in his schemes of colonization. When the trade monopoly was withdrawn from De Monts and his company as autocratically as it had been bestowed, and the unfortunate nobleman saw himself threatened with ruin, Champlain persuaded him that the favor of princes was not the only road to prosperity in the New World, and that individual effort, combined with cohesive construction, might stand clear of the ceaseless intrigue which swayed the French court. This belief eventually took form in the Company of One Hundred Associates which for years controlled the fur trade of Canada.

In the spring of 1608 Champlain and Pontgravé, backed by the staunch De Monts, made final choice of Quebec as a site for the new colony. "I selected," wrote Champlain, "a spot where the river was narrowest, and there I began to clear away the forest, build huts, and cultivate the land." The fitness of this sheltered spot for a trading station was plain to his experienced eye, and it was with absolute certainty that he laid the foundations of a settlement destined to grow into a valorous and supremely beautiful city where his memory is held sacred and dear.

It was a harsh life the settlers led, but sweet with a freedom which the civilizations of the world denied. They traded successfully with the neighboring Hurons and Algonquins, skirmished with the Iroquois who were unfriendly always, and followed the waterways which took them far into northern New York. In 1610 Champlain discovered the lake which bears his name. In 1615 he made his way to Lake Ontario, and to the Lake of the Hurons, where Père le Casson, a Récollet priest, had established a mission. He wintered on the shores of Georgian Bay, and spent forty days getting back to Quebec in the spring. Traveling was slow work in New France.

Champlain's letters, written largely to encourage emigration, are full of zeal, and empty of illusions. He finds much to praise in the wilderness which surrounds him. The soil is fair, the hunting good, the fishing unsurpassed. The berries, especially the blueberries, "a small fruit, but very good to eat," delight him. He says that the squaws dried them for winter use, but nowhere else do we find any record of this housewifely proceeding. The missionaries all agree that the hungry savages gobbled up their fruit as soon as it was ripe, and very often before it had had time to ripen. Wild grapes and wild plums were much to Champlain's fancy, crabapples he ate without enthusiasm, and he even tried to eat May apples, being unwilling that anything which resembled fruit should go to waste.

With the Indians—always excepting the Iroquois—Champlain managed to keep on excellent terms. He traveled far and wide in their company, without confidence, but without fear, and without mishap. He tells dreadful tales of their cruelty to prisoners, and he deplores the filthiness of their personal habits when he is forced to live in close contact with them; but for their intelligence and superb endurance he has a pioneer's understanding regard. "They have good judgment in all that pertains to their manner of living," he writes; "but one cannot rely on them save cautiously, and standing always on guard. They are inveterate liars. They promise much and perform little."

Champlain's observations correspond generally with the observations of the missionaries as told in the Jesuit *Relations*, those remarkable records which have furnished true and ample material for historians. The lugubrious singing in which the Indians took such pleasure was as little to his liking as it was to the liking of Père Le Jeune or Père Charlevoix. He tells us that in the forest one of his savage guides cut his foot so severely that he fainted from loss of blood. While the French surgeon dressed the wound, the other Indians sang, or rather howled, in chorus, by way of encouraging their companion. "More fortunate than we were, he could not hear them," comments the commander grimly.

Champlain also corroborates the statement of missionaries as to companionate marriage, a custom unusual but not unknown among certain tribes. A girl was permitted to live with several young braves before making choice of a husband. The decision once reached was final unless the woman proved barren, in which case the husband might put her away, and try his luck again. The supreme value of childbearing was fully recognized by these least prolific of savages.

For the rest, Champlain makes bitter complaint of mosquitoes, finding them the "most persistent of insects," which they are; he greatly and rightly admires the canoes, so well fitted to their purpose; he spells the Indian names more wildly than do the missionaries, calling one Algonquin tribe the Otaguottouemins, and two Iroquois tribes the Entouhonorons and the Chouontouarouons; and he writes engagingly of the savages' delicate appreciation of tobacco. They held it to be a semi-sacred thing, dedicated to grave occasions and high purposes. When gathered for council, the braves placed all they had, or all they felt that they could spare, on a bark platter, precisely like an offertory collection, and it was solemnly burned as a fitting sacrifice to the gods. One thing which the missionaries failed to observe was clear to Champlain's penetrating eye. They conceived of the Indians as wretched because they saw only the wretchedness of their lives. Champlain always looked beyond the apparent. "Their existence is miserable as compared with ours," he writes; "but it is satisfactory to them because they have not tasted better, and because they believe that there is none more desirable. They are content among themselves, *having no other ambition than to keep alive.*"

It is a keen intelligence which recognizes the increased value of a threatened life. Men never came to doubt its sweetness until it grew secure. When guarded with infinite pains, and fought for day by day, peril gave it savor, and the mere act of survival became an hourly triumph over fate.

As a matter of fact it was none too easy for Champlain and his handful of Frenchmen to keep alive in the snowbound settlement of Quebec. Crops were scanty, winters were long, the fishing season which brought abundance of food was sometimes sorely delayed. Ever and always the colonists were held back by their leader from quarreling with the surrounding Indians. Ever and always he quoted the words of an Iroquois chief who preached better than he practised: "Peace and trade are one." Ever and always he strove to make headway against the traders of Britain and Holland who wanted no rivals in the field. Ever and always he struggled despairingly with the shifting policies of France. It is true that Henry the Fourth had evinced a keen interest in the colony, had granted Champlain an audience, and had found in him a man after his own stalwart heart. Henry, like all his contemporaries, believed that the New World was a path to the very old world of the Orient; and that the coveted trade with China lay within the colonists' reach. So firmly fixed was this notion in the public mind that a French poet who wrote an ode to Champlain lamented the loss of such a roadway as a consequence of the King's untimely death:

> Had Heaven but left thee longer here below,
> France had been linked to China before now.

The assassination of Henry in 1610 deprived Champlain of a support which was not replaced until sixteen years later when Heaven raised him up a friend in the person of Cardinal Richelieu.

This astute statesman may have believed, with
all his predecessors and with all his contemporaries, in the mythical route to China; but what
interested him more keenly was the fur trade of
Quebec, and the consequent need of strengthening the infant colonies of New France. He it was
who formed the Company of One Hundred
Associates, each member of which contributed
three thousand livres. The list of shareholders
comprised the names of the noblest and richest
in the land, from the cardinal himself and great
noblemen of the court to influential courtesans
and venturesome merchants of Paris. The monopoly of the fur trade, once fluctuating and
disastrous, brought prosperity to Canada and
revenue to France. For forty-two years the
company was the centre of authority, and the
avenue to what these simple habitants called
wealth. When its charter was finally revoked by
Louis the Fourteenth, acting on the advice of
Colbert, its days of usefulness were over, and
better methods had supervened; but in the old
rough, hazardous times it did the work at hand,
and did it passing well. Efficiency and business
methods, as we know them now, formed no part
of the colonists' experience.

The unrelenting foe of French commerce was

the English privateer. Few things in life can have been more agreeable than privateering. Hunters and traders worked hard, braved the bitter cold, and risked their lives daily. Then when the boatload of precious furs sailed for France, the privateer ran it down and robbed it for his country's benefit and his own. The odds were overwhelmingly in his favor, and the reward was great. There was always a war of sorts to justify the deed, and the pirate—who was also a patriot—troubled himself little about anything so casual as a treaty. Indeed treaties succeeded one another so rapidly in those days that some ignorance and a good deal of indifference were noticeable even in higher quarters. When Captain David Kirke, commanding a fleet of six vessels, forced the defenceless Quebec to surrender in 1629, he lost the fruits of his labors by ignoring the Treaty of Suze, signed in the April of that year. Charles the First disavowed his subject's high-handed action, while bestowing on him a baronetcy to show that he bore no ill-will. Quebec was restored to France, and Champlain returned to Canada after the Treaty of St.-Germain-en-Laye. There followed a few years of peace and progress. The successful trading station at Three Rivers was established, the Indians were won back to their allegiance; and settlers, feeling themselves reasonably safe— nothing can be more relative than safety— crossed the sea in reassuring numbers. When Champlain died on Christmas day, 1635, he left to France a colony, small and weak, but steadfast in purpose and of unshaken loyalty. Quebec does well to honor the adventurer whose courage gave her birth, and whose wisdom and patience enabled her to survive.

Parkman says that in Champlain alone we find the life of New France. Strong of will and trained to endurance, hopeful in adversity and cautious in success, keenly observant and quick to draw conclusions, he was essentially the right man in the right place. If his work was hard, his setbacks many, his pleasures few, and his comforts wholly negligible, he was spared, or he spared himself, the lot that falls to many a good man—the discharging of uncongenial duties in an unsympathetic society. He had chosen his own manner of living, and it brought him some glorious hours. We know what these hours were. When he saw the beautiful Falls of Montmorency which he named after the Admiral of France. When he first looked upon the great inland seas. When he descended the La Chine Rapids, being the second white man to accomplish this perilous feat. These were the rapids which wrecked Louis Joliet a half century later. "The water falleth as it were steppe by steppe," wrote Champlain, "and in every place where it hath some small height it maketh a strong boyling with the force and speed of its run."

Champlain's marriage was perhaps the least satisfactory episode of his life. To wed a child of twelve for business reasons is not a likely path to domestic happiness. Hélène Boullé was the daughter of the secretary of the king's chamber. What the duties of the secretary of the king's chamber were is not clear. Probably he had no duties, only emoluments; but his influence was of value to Champlain and De Monts. Boullé was a Huguenot, but the little bride was transformed into a Catholic to meet her husband's views. She remained in France to be educated, and it was a matter of ten years before she crossed the sea to Quebec. What she found there tried her bravery to the utmost. The tradition of her youth, her gentle breeding, and the suggestion of luxury she brought with her,

her silken dress,
And her fragile loveliness,

still lingers in the old city; and a few tales are told of kindness to the savages and the sick.

Champlain was then Lieutenant Governor of New France. His authority was absolute, he gave his wife what meagre comforts he could muster; and the man who enabled his followers to be "cleanly and merry" when shut in by the snows of Acadia must have made conditions bearable in Quebec. But the isolation, the cold, the ever-present hint of danger were more than Hélène could bear. She had apparently no love for her husband, who was eighteen years her senior, to counterbalance the distressfulness of her surroundings. After four years she returned to France, became *dévote*, and as a matter of course wanted to enter a convent. This was not practicable for a married woman unless husband and wife became, with each other's consent, priest and nun; and nothing could have been further from Champlain's thoughts than taking holy orders. In his old age (men grew old at sixty-eight in those days) he resembled Tennyson's Ulysses, restless on the shores of Ithaca:

I am a part of all that I have met;
Yet all experience is an arch wherethro'
Gleams that untravell'd world whose margin fades
For ever and for ever when I move.

It was the pathway to China that Champlain always hoped to find; and it was the Far North (a thing of reality not of dreams) that he keenly desired to behold. From the savages he had heard of Hudson Bay, and his heart was set on seeing for himself "the salt water cutting into the frozen land." But he never succeeded in persuading the Indians about him to undertake the long and perilous voyage. Radisson and Grosseilliers were the first white men to approach Hudson Bay from the land; and Champlain died with longings unfulfilled, but with a brave list of achievements to his credit. The place of his interment is unknown, but Quebec has selected her fairest site on which to raise a monument in his honor. The somewhat swaggering statue that surmounts it turns from the sea to face the fort that he built and the city that he founded. In the library of Dieppe is preserved the manuscript of his early voyage to the West Indies. It was translated and published by the Hakluyt Society in 1859, and contains what was probably the first suggestion of the Panama Canal, "whereby the voyage to the South Sea would be shortened by more than fifteen hundred leagues."

Champlain's portrait, attributed to Balthazar Moncornet, is as apochryphal as Cartier's, and as satisfactory to people not concerned with the formality of facts. If he did not look like that, he should have done so—keen, resolute, and distinguished. His narratives (the first dedicated to Montmorency, the second to Richelieu) are plain, straightforward accounts of New France and of his own labors. They are immaculately free from egotism and self-glorification. His life was one of singular austerity, of devotion to a cause, and of supreme loyalty to his country and his church. His wife, who by virtue of a marriage contract inherited his possessions, entered the Ursuline Order, founded a convent at Meaux, and lived long in the odor of sanctity, and in the heart of civilization. No impulse to revisit Quebec stirred her heart when, four years after Champlain's death, Mère Marie and Mme. de la Peltrie sailed joyously from Dieppe to carry the light of faith and the warmth of charity to the children of the New World.

Chapter V

QUEBEC

WHEN we read Mère Marie's account of the three months' voyage to Quebec we are irresistibly reminded of another journey undertaken by the ever-adventurous Ursulines nearly a century later to New Orleans. *That* trip took five months to a day, and carried with it greater dangers and excitements. The earlier vessel, the *Saint Joseph*, encountered nothing more perilous than an iceberg which loomed out of the fog near enough to threaten its safety. But Mère Marie had barely time to gather her habit closely about her, so that she might drown—if drown she must— "with decency," when the danger was past and no harm done. The later boat, the *Gironde*, encountered every possible disaster save shipwreck. It was swept out of its course by heavy gales, and pursued by pirates; it ran aground near the mouth of the Mississippi, threw overboard its cargo, and lost its livestock. Its passengers lived on short rations of rice, beans cooked with suet, and salt pork. The nuns, who were on their way to open the first convent school in what is now the United States, reached their destination in a forlorn and destitute condition; whereas the Canada-bound pilgrims crossed the sea in comfort and seclusion, their only trouble being the scarcity of drinking water, though there appears to have been plenty of wine.

What really differentiates the two voyages, however, is the contrast between their two annalists. Mère Marie tells her tale quietly and well; but one of the Ursulines who sailed on the *Gironde* chanced to be Madeleine Hachard, a young novice known in the order as Mère Madeleine de Saint Stanislas, and a writer of uncommon vivacity. Her story is a riot of sound and color, of vivid descriptions, and of pure fun. Mère Marie looked most of the time into her own soul. Madeleine's bright eyes were fixed on the transient happenings of each day. Mère Marie was patient and serene under every mischance. Madeleine's high spirits rose to meet catastrophe with something akin to zest. When the badly battered *Gironde* anchored in the harbor of the Belize, the Ursulines had still a week's journey on two small freight boats to reach New Orleans. All day they sat perched precariously on the freight, drenched with rain, and moving with caution lest they should fall into the water. All night they lay on damp mattresses devoured by mosquitoes. Their fare was salt pork and hard tack. Madeleine does not say they bore these things composedly for God's sake; she says they bore them hilariously for the pleasure of talking about them to one another, and of writing about them to friends at home. It must be confessed that, as described in her letters, they do sound vastly amusing.

Mère Marie and Mme. de la Peltrie, more sedate but every whit as courageous, had also a very uncomfortable journey from Tadoussac, where they landed on July 15th, to Quebec, which they did not reach until the first of August. The intervening weeks were spent on a small and very dirty boat laden with salted codfish. The nuns lived on the codfish (there was at least plenty of it), supplemented by ship biscuit. They were most honorably received at Quebec. Guns were fired, shops were closed, and workmen took a holiday to welcome the new arrivals. The governor, Charles Huoult de Montmagny, who had succeeded Champlain, sent a canoe laden with food to the boat, so that the poor ladies should not be too hungry when they landed. He met them on the dock with a small company of soldiers and priests. Mass was sung in the chapel of Notre-Dame de la Recouvrance which Champlain had built, and where he was in all probability buried. The hospital was visited, dinner was served in the fort, and then the Ursulines were ceremoniously conducted to the shack that had been prepared for them under the shelter of the cliff which rose steeply and beautifully to the wooded highlands beyond.

It was a humble dwelling place, comprising two fair rooms, an attic, and a little chapel of planks and rough plastering. Mère Saint Joseph, who was called the "laughing nun" because of her insistent gayety, christened it "the Louvre," by which name it was known in the community. The day after landing, the nuns and Mme. de la Peltrie, escorted by Père Le Jeune and Père Vimont, visited the mission of Sillery, a few miles from Quebec. It owed its existence to the Chevalier Noël Brulard de Sillery, Knight of Malta, a gentleman of wealth who held office in the French court. Deeply moved by the needs of New France, he resolved to devote his fortune to founding missions in the wilderness. The one that bore his name was the first and most important of these, and there stood until twenty years ago an old stone house whose walls defied decay, and part of which was the Jesuits' headquarters in 1640.

Sillery, when visited by the Ursulines, was a cheerful spot with a tiny church of its own, and a still tinier hospital. The Algonquin huts clustered closely within the inadequate protection of a palisade, and the surrounding fields were under fair cultivation. The dream of the early missionaries was to turn the savages into home-staying, housekeeping agriculturists; and it was many a long year before they learned that the red men, unlike the black men, could never be lured or driven into domestication. Mère Marie had all the hopefulness of the inexperienced, and Mme. de la Peltrie's mounting enthusiasm impelled her to embrace every little Indian she encountered; indifferent alike, remarked Père Le Jeune, to the dirt of the child, or to its wonderment at such embraces, kissing not being customary among the savages. They were habitually "cold in greeting."

The ship that brought the nuns to Quebec brought also the welcome news of the birth of the Dauphin, afterwards Louis the Fourteenth. These tidings, received with joy, proved to be in the end really and truly joyful, inasmuch as Louis was the one and only French king who took a keen, lasting, and helpful interest in the American colonies. As the colonists could not foresee this happy circumstance, their delight seems a trifle exaggerated; but life was dull in New France, and its inhabitants lost no chance to diversify and enliven it. "No sooner had the word 'Dauphin' escaped the lips of the messengers," wrote Père Le Jeune, "than joy entered into our hearts and thanksgiving into our souls. The news spread everywhere; the *Te Deum Laudamus* was chanted, and bonfires and fireworks were prepared with every device possible in these countries."

On the 15th of August, the Feast of the Assumption, a procession in honor of the Blessed Virgin and in thanksgiving for the royal infant, marched to Notre-Dame de la Recouvrance. Heading it were six Indian youths dressed in costumes sent by the French court, scarlet satin, velvet, and cloth of gold. They carried themselves proudly and with grave dignity. After them came Mme. de la Peltrie (how she must have enjoyed it!) with four little Indian girls, also in French dress. The governor, his staff, the missionaries, and all the colonists walked in the procession, "without any other order than that suggested by humility." The nuns alone were denied this pleasant privilege. To make amends, the ranks halted before the hospital and before

the humble convent, while their inmates sang
the *Exaudiat*—"to the delight of our savages,"
comments the missionary proudly.

A vesper service closed the day, after which
the Frenchmen, priests and laity, would have
been glad to go to bed; but the tireless Indians
assembled for a council. The governor urbanely
attended, bringing Mme. de la Peltrie with him;
and the weary Jesuits, knowing that speech-
making was dear to the savage heart, prepared
themselves to listen and respond. Inattention
on these august occasions was an unpardonable
offense. "Be wise and hearken," said a chief
warningly to Père Le Jeune who perhaps looked
sleepy; "let not thy mind wander, lest thou
shouldst lose a word of what I am about to say."

He did have a good deal to say, and so did
other Algonquins. Mme. de la Peltrie was so
moved by their recountal of scant crops and long
winter fasts that she begged Père Vimont to
assure them that if she could help to dig and
plant with her own hands she would gladly do so;
to which a saturnine savage replied that corn
planted by arms so weak would be late in ripening. The council concluded with the presentation
of a little Indian dress as a gift for the Dauphin.
The spokesman said that they did not expect

the great king's son to wear it, but that they thought it might please him to know how the children of the forests were clad.

If Louis, a king at five, resembled other little boys, this artless gift would probably have become his most precious possession. But it never went to France. Smallpox was rife among the Indians, and the missionaries feared lest any product of their hands should carry contagion. No words can adequately describe the ravages of this disease among a people habitually filthy, and ignorant of the simplest rules of sanitation. It was said that smallpox killed as many Hurons as did the Iroquois. Strange and dreadful tales were told of lonely deaths, of blind terror, of helpless devotion, and of stolid cruelty. An Indian woman, whose son and brother were ill, resolved to carry her son to Quebec, a journey of several days. As there was no room in the canoe for her brother, she brained him with a club. His young son and daughter begged her to take them with her, lest they should starve in the forest. She bade the boy kill his little sister, saying she could not take both. This he did, the child submitting quietly to the inevitable. The three survivors reached Quebec, where mother and son died in the hospital. The boy lived to tell the tale, and subsequently returned to his tribe. The smallpox, which had been a threat in August, became a deadly certainty in September. The hospital being filled to overflowing, it was necessary for the Ursulines to take the children under their care. The little French girls who were waiting to be taught must wait longer while the little savages were nursed. It was the experience of Milan repeated, but with this difference: Milan was a big and rich city where all that was wanted could be procured. Quebec was a settlement of two hundred and fifty colonists, dependent for its needs upon France. Beds there were none in the convent, and the mattresses were laid so close together on the floor that the nuns had to step over one sick child to reach another. They used up their house linen, their body linen, even the available portions of their habits, to make bandages. Their neighbors gave them what help they could, and Mme. de la Peltrie and Charlotte Barré worked valiantly, no task being too hard or too repulsive for their hands. One comfort they had. The Indians were the most docile and uncomplaining of patients. This was also the experience of the nursing nuns. The savages suffered silently and died composedly. Many of those in the hospital did die, alas, while the Ursulines lost only four children, an incredibly small number.

It may seem strange that none of Mère Marie's little sisterhood caught the infection; but so it often happens in times of stress and strain. Readers of Lady Inglis's *Siege of Lucknow* will remember that this intrepid lady fell ill of smallpox in the early days of the assault. She could not be removed from the crowded Residency because there was no other place of safety. She could not be isolated because there was no room for isolation. She saw her friends, and heard the tragic news as it came in hour by hour. She recovered, and no one took the disease. In those days of peril and catastrophe nobody had time to catch a disease. So it was with the Ursulines. Like Hotspur, they lacked the leisure to be sick.

It was February before the epidemic had spent itself, and peace was restored to the colony. The exhausted nuns were urged by Père Le Jeune to begin at once the study of the Indian languages. They obeyed with more good-will than energy. Mère Marie found it uphill work. She said the Indian words rolled like stones in her head, bruising it; and she, who became in time so proficient, despaired at first of proficiency. The "laughing nun" made the most rapid progress,

and was soon able to speak the Huron tongue
with a fair degree of fluency. As the spring advanced, life grew easier and more agreeable. The
ships from France brought fresh stores to the
convent. The dilapidated habits were once
again made *convenable*. For the first time since
their arrival these devoted exiles could take stock
of their circumstances and surroundings.

What did they think of both? When the
Ursulines of New Orleans had completed their
horrid journey, they found awaiting them a
comfortable home, and a land flowing with milk
and honey. Madeleine Hachard, blessed with
the appetite of youth, is loud in her praises of
the good food provided by the bounteous hand
of Nature and the supreme genius of the black
cooks. Even the little cat that had joined the
community in France, "confident that there were
plenty of mice in Louisiana," enjoyed a diversi-
fied diet. But Quebec, small and bleak, offered
no such carnal delights. Nature was niggardly of
everything except rock and river and sea. The
Indians could not cook, and would not serve.
Life was primitive, and would have been rude
save for the imperishable amenities of French
civilization.

It was greatly to Mère Marie's credit that she

recognized the beauty of her surroundings. The cult of Nature worship was then unknown; and where Nature is inimical to man, she has never been greatly beloved. Wordsworth's Nature, it may be observed, was beneficent. What he saw about him was the "moral scenery" for which Hannah More felt a patronizing regard. But in New France Nature carried a perpetual threat. Even Champlain looked at her askance. He was too great a navigator not to admire the superb rush of the Saguenay River, its depth and its velocity; but as for its shores, at which tourists now gape rapturously, he found them "very disagreeable from whatever point of view" —a verdict pleasurably suggestive of Horace Walpole's "high and horrid Alps."

Yet Mère Marie, who had left the loveliness of Touraine, the charming moderation of its revolving seasons, "*son climat supple et chaud,*" wrote George Sand, "*ses pluies abondantes et courtes,*" knew that the cruel and glittering world which surrounded her was a world of beauty. The convent, with its back to the rock and its face to the sea, commanded an enchanting prospect; the pure keen air kept the nuns in good health, and made them hungry for the salted fish, salted pork, and sagamité which formed the staple of

moccasin in the soup pot. This last mishap suggests a very unusual sense of humor on the part of a misguided Indian child.

As for the cold, it seems to have amazed Mère Marie more than it distressed her. A lifetime spent in the heart of France had done little to prepare her for such an experience. If she and her sisterhood could have gone outdoors and braved the buffeting wind, they might have warmed their frozen blood, and rejoiced in defying the elements. But caged in their little house, they could do nothing but hug the fire. "Do not suppose," wrote their superior to the convent in Tours, "that we could live long without returning again and again to the fireplace. Even I, who have never wanted to warm myself, am now reluctant to leave it." To pray in the freezing chapel was impossible. The rosary was recited and the office read in the community room, which was a community room only when it was not needed for a dozen other purposes. Private devotions were deferred until the tired and sleepy nuns were in bed. Mère Marie considered with Saint Theresa that acute physical discomfort was incompatible with absorption in prayer. Now and then she expressed concern about the Jesuits who were always in danger of having their fingers and ears frozen, and who seemed insufficiently aware of the fact. Now and then she heard and repeated tragic tales of *coureurs de bois* who were lost in the deep snows. And not *coureurs de bois* only. During her second winter in Quebec a manservant in the house of one of her neighbors was overcome by the cold when returning late at night, and perished alone in the darkness. Nature's primeval cruelty was a fit setting for the cruelty of her savage sons.

Chapter VI

IN DAYS OF PEACE

Two things were apparent from the start to Mère Marie's practised eye: the absurd inadequacy of the "Louvre" to the work she had on hand, and the absurd inadequacy of Mme. de la Peltrie's income when it came to building in Quebec. This generous lady could do no more than pay the running expenses of the convent, and assist the mission at Sillery; she could spare no capital for the erection of a new house. Therefore it was that Mère Marie discovered, like the head of any modern institution, that her most pressing and most formidable task was the raising of funds.

Naturally these funds could be raised only in France. The colonists had no money, but Quebec gave what she had to give—ground. The governor was authorized by the Company of One Hundred Associates to assign to the Ursulines six arpents—about nine acres—of cleared land in what was later called the upper town. The site was chosen for its comparative safety, being under the protection of the fort. The foundation stone was laid by Mme. de la Peltrie in the spring of 1640, and Mère Marie set herself resolutely to the business of writing the most persuasive begging letters of her day.

At first these letters went to Ursuline convents which could be depended upon for interest and sympathy. Then they found their way to other communities rich enough to be begged from. Gradually their area widened until it embraced some of the most important people in France: clerics, prelates, men of affairs, and women of rank and fashion. All seem to have been impressed by the practical intelligence of this secluded nun whose energy never flagged, and who carried every undertaking to a successful and legitimate close.

It was not the education of French children that Mère Marie stressed in her appeals; that was easy and assured. It was the civilizing and Christianizing of little Indians that she urged with all the fervor of her heart, and with every argument that might carry conviction. She reminded her readers over and over again that the good-will and affection of these convent-taught girls helped to preserve friendly relations when they returned to their tribes. She affirmed that, if well trained, they made good wives for the French colonists; faithful, obedient, and in-

dustrious. Miscegenation, that deadly crime in
our slave-holding states, was esteemed in New
France as a sensible solution of its most pressing
problem, the perpetual need of wives. Above
and beyond all, Mère Marie asked help in bringing heathen children into the fold of Christ, and
this plea never failed. The simple belief of that
simple day held faith to be a gift from God which
Christians should cherish gratefully and share
generously. Even men who were no better than
their neighbors, and women who were no better
than they should be (there were many such in
Paris and Touraine), clung firmly to this creed.
The combination of an over-developed moral
sense and an undeveloped spiritual sense, which
Matthew Arnold found so distressing in Nine-
teenth Century England, was noticeably lacking
in Seventeenth Century France.

So the money poured in, and the walls of the
new convent rose high. The stone was quarried
near by, and Quebec supplied the sand and brick;
but the artisans—builders, plasterers, and carpenters—were brought from France. They were
engaged for three years, and their average wage
was thirty cents a day, which Mère Marie
thought high, especially as she had to provide
their food, "even on Sundays, feast days, and in

bad weather." The three-story building was ninety-two feet long, and twenty-eight feet deep. Four great fireplaces burned a hundred and seventy-five cords of wood in a winter with very indifferent results. The nuns, being fairly crowded out of the "Louvre," took possession of their new abode before it was finished, exulting in its spaciousness, and in the blessed privacy of cells. Their numbers had increased, but their work was harder and heavier. Père Le Jeune, inordinately proud of the handsome structure, wrote to France that it was "the fairest ornament of the colony, and a marked help in the detention and conversion of the savages." Even Mère Marie was moved to elation by its manifest merits, her only regret being the size of the chapel. "You would think it very small," she told her son, "but it is impossible to heat a bigger one."

An old sketch of this much-vaunted edifice shows it to have been severely plain, with four stout chimneys, and

A little cupola more neat than solemn

for its only ornament. A well-curb marks the place where the nuns obtained "their excellent supply of water." A tall paling surrounds the house and grounds. Outside this paling is Mme. de la Peltrie's modest abode. Also two picturesque wigwams, added evidently by the artist under the mistaken impression that he was giving local color to the scene.

It was to be expected that Mère Marie should emphasize in her letters the beneficent results of her labors, that she should paint in glowing colors the piety and good behavior of the little Indians whom she taught. The *Relations* took the same tone with the same naïveté and fervor. It must be admitted that the tales told by priests and nuns bear a singular resemblance to the tales told by Cotton Mather and his contemporaries for the edification of Puritan readers: "Some examples of Children in several parts of New England, in whom the fear of God was remarkably Budding before they died." "A Particular Account of Some Extraordinary Pious Motions and devout Exercises observed of late in many Children in Siberia."

If the little Puritans were good because they had to be, the little Indians—or at least the little Indian girls—were good because generations of docility lay behind them. "This docility is common to all from seven to seventeen," wrote

Mère Marie. Moreover, silence was natural to them, and in all the convent schools of the world silence is, and has always been, an overestimated virtue. Père Vimont admitted that Indian children never fidgeted, or played, or whispered in church, as French children were sometimes wont to do. They sat still, or knelt motionless, obedient to instruction, and presenting an edifying spectacle.

Savages are apt to be imitative. Mère Marie's little savages took to pious practices like little ducks to water. They told their beads, they sang hymns lustily, they delighted in going to confession, and in reminding one another of faults that should be confessed; they were so rigorously observant in performing small acts of devotion that even the gratified nuns were known to sigh over their excessive zeal. Yet the three children who wanted to be hermits, and who retired into the garden to lead lives of solitude and prayer (until the sound of the dinner bell recalled them to the world), were not unlike the little Theresa of Avila, who essayed with her brother's help to build a hermitage, and who was defeated in her pious purpose by the smallness of the stones, and her lack of structural skill.

One wayward impulse remained in the hearts of these phlegmatic pupils. They were subject to spells of passionate nostalgia, and sickened for the life of the woods. Nothing could hold them back when this desire was upon them. They would slip away by day or night, and seek the shelter of their miserable homes, sometimes many miles away. The nuns christened these fugitives "*petites coureuses de bois*," and tried hard to close their gates when, after a few days or a few weeks, they invariably returned to the convent. But their determination to get in was equal to their determination to get out. They would crouch quietly at the door for five, ten, or twenty hours; pitiful little objects, cold, hungry, and forlorn, confident that by patient waiting they could wear out the resistance of authority.

It is noticeable that Mme. de la Peltrie found the Indian children affectionate and demonstrative. She seems to have broken down their barriers of reserve, and they accepted her as though she had been one of themselves. They were rather lovable little creatures when they were washed, and kept washed. Mme. de la Peltrie scrubbed and combed them energetically, made them frocks of which they were inordinately proud ("they had not been used to seeing

themselves so fine"), taught them to sew, heard
them recite their catechism, and played with
them in the convent garden. Close contact with
these little savages was in no way disagreeable
to her, and she let them put their arms around
her and press close to her knees. The "laughing
nun" was her only rival in their affection. Mère
Saint Joseph spoke the Huron tongue, Mme. de
la Peltrie became fairly conversant with the
Montagnais, and the Indian "seminarians"
(a dignified term) picked up French with the
facile ease of childhood.

They also acquired a gentleness of manner
which gave the Ursulines (ladies well-born and
well-bred) justifiable pleasure. They mingled
freely with the French children, though they
were taught apart, and they observed closely
all that went on about them. Mère Marie wrote
to the convent in Tours that one little Indian
girl, Madeleine Amiskoueian, behaved as though
she had been born and bred in Touraine; and
that another, Marie Negabamat, became "more
accomplished every day." She told her corre-
spondent that the nuns served the sagamité to
visiting Indians in bowls of wood or bark; and
that the hungry guests, finding that spoons were
scarce, or that eating with them was slow work,

would sometimes pick up a bowl by its "ears,"
and devour its contents greedily and at ease.
Those of us who in our childhood read Miss
Edgeworth's most idyllic story, *Simple Susan*,
will recall a somewhat similar situation. The
seminarians, however, were never guilty of such
an indecorum. "Our pupils are more polite,"
commented Mère Marie proudly. "Being in our
company has made them so."

One more result of education deserves to be
chronicled. The little Indian girls, clean and
supercilious, refused to play with the little
Indian boys who occasionally came to the convent with their mothers, and who were both
amazed and chagrined at such treatment. They
were equally averse to coming into familiar
contact with Indian men. Parkman, who takes
note of this circumstance, attributes it to prudish-
ness, to a precocious sex-consciousness, fostered
by the teaching of the nuns. But looked at less
superficially, it seems like a natural reaction
against an age-old tyranny of which these
children were becoming dimly aware. They had
seen their mothers treated like beasts of burden
("women are the Indians' mules," observed
Champlain crisply), and they had seen the
dignified lives of the nuns, whose work, if hard,

was of their own volition. When they said childishly that they wanted to stay always in the convent, they were probably not thinking about the grace of virginity, but about the pleasures of decency and freedom. They were little unconscious feminists, and feminism being then untabulated, their distaste for boys and men was regarded as an excess of modesty.

In fact Indian marriages offered to the missionaries a broad field of perplexity. Divorce was easy and common, but polygamy was rare. When practised, it was not for amorous delight, but for utilitarian purposes. A brave who desired baptism explained painstakingly to the priest that he could not put away either of his wives because his cleared land needed the labor of two women. He was a kind-hearted young man who did not want to overwork one wife; therefore he kept a couple. Another Indian, who had been baptized, asked to be married in Lent. When told to wait until Easter, he said it was impossible because his cornfield was ready to be planted: "It is not the custom of our people to put women to work until we have married them," he said with a touch of chivalry.

The only indulgence granted to squaws was a share in the torture of captives. This was

a highly esteemed privilege, and they showed a
hideous ingenuity in prolonging the hours of
pain. But the first lesson taught to converts
was that cruelty was a deadly sin; and while
adults were usually unpersuadable (the traditions of their race held fast), children were
turned aside forever from the great national
pastime.

Before the Ursulines had been a year in their
new home, something happened which made
Mère Marie profoundly grateful that she was
drawing help from France. Mme. de la Peltrie
went to Montreal. The impulse which carried
her thither was as disinterested as the impulse
which had brought her to Quebec; but impulsive-
ness, however noble, is apt to be fraught with
inconvenience to somebody. The founding of
Montreal ranks high in the history of heroism.
It was a savage spot, perilously close to the
lands of the Iroquois, and frequented only by a
few intrepid traders. Jacques Cartier had reached
it, and had given the name of Mont Royal to
the rocky eminence which overhung the island.
Champlain had noted the value of the site—
between two navigable rivers—as a trading
station. But it was left for Paul de Chomedey,
Sieur de Maisonneuve, an able soldier and a

devout Catholic, to lay the foundation of this stately city, which English writers (meaning to be complimentary) have called the Birmingham of Canada.

Its first conception was due to the enthusiasm of Jérôme le Royer de la Dauversière, a gentleman of good birth who was receiver of taxes in Anjou. His avocation was prosaic, his family large and exacting; but he himself was a mystic, an ascetic, a dreamer of dreams. His overwhelming desire to plant a mission in New France was ably seconded by a young priest, Jean Jacques Olier, who subsequently founded the Seminary of St. Sulpice in Paris. With the help of friends they established the Society of Notre-Dame de Mont Royal, raised funds, and organized an expedition under the leadership of Maisonneuve. With it went two women, one of them Mlle. Jeanne Mance, who was to play a notable part in the history of Ville Marie de Mont Royal, by which name the settlement was first known.

The pilgrims reached Quebec too late in the autumn to risk ascending the St. Lawrence. They wintered in the home of M. Puiseaux near Sillery; and Mme. de la Peltrie became possessed by the desire to accompany Mlle. Mance to wilder scenes and greater perils than Quebec could

offer. To a spirit like hers danger had charms
which prolonged discomfort lacked, and the
duty that was close at hand was commonplace
by comparison with labors more remote. When,
on the 8th of May, Maisonneuve and his party
embarked at St. Michel in a flat-bottomed boat
with sails and two large canoes, Mme. de le
Peltrie went with them. Also Père Vimont, fully
alive to the importance of the new mission, and
Montmagny who, as governor, felt bound to see
how the adventure, of which he disapproved, was
conducted. An official's life in New France was
not an easy one. Ten days were consumed in the
journey, and on the 18th the little fleet glided
alongside of a meadow where early flowers were
blooming. In this green field an altar was quickly
raised. Mme. de la Peltrie and Charlotte Barré
decorated it with ready art, and Père Vimont
said the first Mass on the site of Montreal.

Meanwhile the Ursulines, bereft of Mme. de
la Peltrie's liberal assistance, had a hard time
fulfilling their obligations. "Temporalities, or
the lack of them, retard the spiritualities," commented Père Le Jeune sadly. It was characteristic
of Mère Marie that she made no complaint,
asked for no consideration, aired no grievance.
She illustrated Saint Theresa's axiom, "Where

virtue is well rooted, provocations matter little."
If, like the Spanish nun, she ardently desired
clean linen and good manners, she was prepared,
if need be, to do without the linen, and confine
herself to the less expensive luxury, the only one,
it is said, that Saint Francis permitted to his
poverty.

Perhaps, knowing Mme. de la Peltrie as she
did, Mère Marie considered her return to Quebec as more than likely. This hope, if she entertained it, was well founded. During the eighteen
months spent by the fugitive in Ville Marie she
found no work fitted to her hand. Jeanne Mance
took into her tiny cabin a sick settler or a
wounded Indian, and nursed him back to health.
When money was sent her for a hospital, she was
compelled to spend it in defenses against the
Iroquois. Otherwise there would have been no
need for a hospital; a graveyard would have sufficed. For seventeen years this brave lady devoted herself to the care of the suffering, and
her name has not been forgotten by the city
that she served. Montreal has dedicated to her
honor a street, a park, and a monument; and she
deserves them all.

Life in this remote and imperiled settlement
was terribly hard. Maisonneuve had fortified it

as strongly as he could, but all who ventured beyond the protection of its fort were in hourly danger. Six Frenchmen were surprised by the Iroquois while hewing timber in the woods. Three were slain, and three carried away as captives. Of these one managed to escape; the other two were burned. The Hurons were friendly if they felt it safe to be so, but false when fear smote their hearts. Outside the cleared fields the blackness of the forest held tragic possibilities. Even the traders came stealthily to this hidden spot, and left it with what speed they could. Compared to it, Quebec was an abode of comfort and security.

To Quebec Mme. de la Peltrie returned; but not until after she had sought, and sought in vain, for permission to visit one of the Huron missions. She ardently desired to come into closer relations with the savages, and to try her hand at their conversion. The Jesuits firmly refused to consider this wild project. Life in the missions was hard enough and hazardous enough without the complication of a woman's presence. They intimated that there was work and to spare in Quebec for a dozen intelligent women, but that the outposts belonged to men.

When, after an absence of a year and a half,

Mme. de la Peltrie went back to her empty house and her abandoned friends, she was welcomed with warmth by Mère Marie, and with genuine delight by the little Indians who had not forgotten their kind friend and playmate. She never again left them, and never relaxed her charities in their behalf. It was her especial pleasure to provide a modest trousseau and a small sum of money for any one of them who married a baptized Indian, and this circumstance greatly enhanced their value in the eyes of eligible young braves. When her faithful follower, Charlotte Barré, entered the convent, she gave her a dowry of three thousand livres; a charming act of generosity on her part, because the loss of companionship left her very lonely. About this time she adopted a semi-religious dress, less severe and more becoming than a habit, and this dress was her nearest approach to a "vocation." Devout as a nun, devoted as a nun, she remained a free lance to the end.

Quebec was growing fast. Forty French families crossed the sea, and settled within its borders. Food, of a sort, was more plentiful, and safety seemed assured. If water in the casks froze every winter night, which was a trial, the

St. Lawrence was for two winters so hard frozen that Indians ran swiftly over the ice "as though it had been a meadow"; and this the colonists thought a beautiful sight. It seems appalling to us now to consider how largely eels figured in their diet; but the monks of the Middle Ages, who have been reproached unduly for luxurious habits, had little else to eat in Lent. Eels are as nourishing as they are loathsome. Père le Mercier, who writes of them enthusiastically as the "manna" of the habitants, would have us believe that the eels of New France were of a finer flavor than the eels of old France, besides being bigger and fatter. Père Vimont says that from the beginning of September until the end of October they were so abundant in the St. Lawrence that all the French and all the Indians were busy catching them in enormous quantities. The French fished for them by day, the Indians speared them at night by torchlight, a strange and picturesque spectacle. The French salted them for winter use, the Indians, who ate no salt, dried them in the smoke. The stench from the drying eels and rotting refuse carried far, but the savages were indifferent to stenches. They stored away their dried eels in dirty heaps, and made sure that they would not perish of hunger in the winter, a matter of infinite importance.

As the colony grew stronger, it grew gayer, brighter, and more social. Once tolerably sure of the necessities of life, it strove with instinctive ardor for the amenities. It even—being French—wanted to be amused. A few years later this desire would have found expression in rudely staged dramas and ballets; but under Montmagny's ascetic rule a ballet was unthinkable, and a drama was perforce of a semi-religious character. Ardent play lovers, however, are not easily discouraged; and a "tragi-comic" morality was given with so much spirit that we read in the *Relations* of the amazement it caused. Spectators could not believe that such good actors would have been found among gentlemen unacquainted with the stage. The Sieur Martial Piraubé distinguished himself above all others; but we are not told what manner of part he played. The governor desired that something which might edify and instruct the savages should be tacked on to the performance. Accordingly it closed with a spectacle in which the soul of a sinner was pursued by two demons, and hurled into the mouth of a highly realistic hell which belched out flames to receive them. By way of driving the lesson home, both sinner and demons spoke the Algonquin tongue. This representation may have appeared comical to the French; but the unhumorous Indians received it with serious and satisfactory solicitude.

Other signs and tokens point to the comparative well-being of the colony. In the convent the French scholars increased rapidly. Mère Marie wrote to her son that M. de Repentigny, whose little daughters were pensionnaires, was about to visit France, and would bring him good news of her. The number of Indian children was limited only by the capacity of the house to receive them. The services of the Church were conducted with decent solemnity. In the hospital the ceremony of washing the feet of poor patients on Holy Thursday was religiously observed. The governor, surrounded by his most distinguished associates, washed the feet of the Indian men. French ladies washed the feet of the Indian women "very lovingly and reverently." It is on record in the *Journal des Jésuites* that the Ursulines found time during Lent to paint an altar cloth for the parish church, and that on Christmas Day, 1645, they gave "a noble length of cloth to the French and savage poor." The Jes-

uits made a great baking for that day, and distributed many loaves of bread. They discovered
later that the Indians exchanged this good bread
—a luxury to which they were unaccustomed—
for things they needed more. The nuns made
pastry for the priests' Christmas dinner; not
childish tarts, but a substantial and well-gar-
nished pâté of venison, the most attainable of
winter meats. On New Year's Day they cooked
and sent to these ill-fed clerics "a perfect banquet"; but we do not know what constituted a
banquet in times when a daily meal meant salted
fish and porridge.

For if everybody was open-handed, everybody was likewise poor. Economy and liberality,
plainness and nicety went hand in hand. When
Mlle. Gifford, the very young daughter of an
official, was married to M. Maure, she gratefully accepted from the Jesuits the remnants of
an old but fine cassock, "to line a pair of sleeves."
But we also read that when Mlle. Couillar married the son of Jean Guion in the Church of
Notre-Dame de la Recouvrance, "there were two
violins for the first time." Richness of temperament is the salvation of the pioneer who is
necessarily poor in goods. Quebec had dark
days ahead of her; but when she listened to those

violins she knew that the first bitter struggle for existence was over. She had begun to be conscious of pleasures that exceeded the mere joy of survival.

Chapter VII

IN DAYS OF WAR

SANTAYANA's tragic finality, "Only the dead have seen the end of war," was an article of faith in New France. As in the Middle Ages, war was more normal than peace. There were weeks of respite, there were months of tranquillity, there was occasionally a whole unruffled year; but of permanent concord there was none. In Quebec life went on with hardy composure; in the wilderness savage fought with savage as beast fights with beast, and the white man survived, when he did survive, by a series of dramatic reprieves. The rector of the Jesuit college in Rennes was called to his door to speak to a poor wanderer, shabby, bent, and broken. "You come from New France," said the priest, "do you know anything of Jogues? He was taken by the Iroquois. Is he dead?" And the ragged spectre, lifting his mutilated hands, answered, "I am Jogues."

News traveled slowly from village to village, from mission to mission. Traders carried it,

Indians carried it, sometimes a captive, escaped as by a miracle, brought evil tidings, and showed his scarred body as proof thereof. If the Iroquois surpassed all other tribes in ferocity, their foes did not err on the side of gentleness. A Soco-quiois warrior, who had suffered hours of torture, was brought to the hospital at Sillery. His unhealed sores sickened surgeon and nurse; but the savages crowded about his bed, and gazed at him with absorbed attention. "He bore the dressing of his wounds without saying a word, or giving any indication of pain," wrote Père Le Jeune. "He made known by signs the manner in which they had been inflicted; but he showed no anger or resentment against those who had ill-treated him." The nuns nursed the poor wretch back into the semblance of manhood; but they could not hide the scars, or make his severed fingers grow again.

Mère Marie de Saint Ignace was then head of the new hospital which had been built at Sillery. The site was an inconvenient one for all save the Indian patients, but they were the people whom it was meant to serve. "The French, when ill, have no difficulty in going to Sillery," wrote Père Le Jeune, "but the sick Savages are unable to go to Quebec." The work, always heavy, was augmented by the deepening hostility of the Iroquois, who "prowled all about," and were as dangerous to encounter as prowling tigers in the jungle. In 1643 the hospital had over a hundred Indian patients, besides a number of French workmen ill of a mysterious fever which was first observed at Fort Richelieu, and was known as *mal de terre*. The need of supplies was acute and chronic. The hospital could not organize a "drive" when nobody had any money, and it could not rent rooms at princely rates for the same reason. Besides it had no rooms that were not shared in common.

What it could and did do was to send to France "Lists and Memorandums of Necessaries," which comprised every drug known to that day, and every article which might be of service. Rhubarb and jalap, aloes and incense, lancets and holy-water stoups, white vitriol and yellow wax, balm and ointments, linen to make shirts for the living and shrouds for the dead, needles, scissors, basins, and the *Journée Chrétienne*. These things and many others were to be sent to M. Cramoisy, "Printer in Ordinary to the King," and publisher of the *Relations*, who generously undertook to forward them to Quebec. The careless old phrase, "When my ship comes in," held a world of meaning for the Canadian colonists.

The death of Richelieu was a heavy blow to the pioneers whose hardihood he had admired, and whose interests he had never ceased to serve. The king, who had possessed the negative merit of docility, followed him to the grave. Louis the Fourteenth was a young child. His mother, Anne of Austria, was the least capable of regents, and Mazarin was the most hated of ministers. Between them they emptied the treasury which Richelieu had filled. Well might Père Le Jeune write that New France melted into tears at the ill news which reached her when she most needed encouragement. Well might he wonder how she could pay her way and fight her battles without help. Well might he rejoice in the elemental instinct which makes men on the ragged edge of civilization find delight in facing dangers and overcoming obstacles. And well he knew that this instinct would not grow atrophied from inaction.

The same spirit in a different guise animated the Ursulines shut up in their convent, and deeply aware of everything that was happening around them, as are all people who do not go abroad. They are invariably the first to hear news. Mère Marie was supremely capable of facing emergencies. She was not only remote from fear—many women are that—but she was remote from that sense of disturbance which often nullifies courage. She was fortified against assault. Her love for New France grew with every year of successful work. She speaks of it in a letter as "*cette bienheureuse terre*," and she writes charmingly to the superior at Tours: "We see ourselves here under the necessity of becoming saints. We must consent to this change, or perish."

Nevertheless, when summoning recruits (whom she never failed to get), this wise administrator invariably told them that they must die to the world they knew in order to live in the world which awaited them. That they were fairly successful in doing this is evinced by the fact that in eleven years only one young nun begged to be sent back to her French convent. Her request was immediately granted. Père Vimont says in the *Relations* that so many Ursulines were eager to come to Quebec that he believes the eleven thousand virgins could have been duplicated, and he adds sapiently: "We have room in our colony for only a few religious, but could spend a great deal more money if our friends would kindly send it to us."

It was sent with ungrudging liberality. Also vestments and silver vessels for the altar. Also an abundant supply of woolen and linen cloths, and such highly prized luxuries as prunes, raisins, and dried cherries. The new nuns came from different parts of France, and there was then a diversity of rule as well as a diversity of dress in the scattered Ursuline convents. It was Mère Marie's task to arbitrate these differences, to promote concessions, to adjust and readjust points of dispute, to make clear what was essential and what was not, to insure the harmony and accord which are indispensable to communal life. Six years was the term of a superior's office. Mère Saint Athanase was elected to follow Mère Marie, and the two nuns succeeded each other while they lived. It was a pure formality. Mère Saint Athanase might be the nominal head of the convent, but Mère Marie ruled it. Whether on the throne, or the power behind the throne, the control and the responsibility were hers. Mère Saint Joseph came near to being elected in 1645; but the "laughing nun," serious enough in the face of such an emergency, pleaded to be left with her Indian children. She was the right woman in the right place, and she knew it. "I believe," wrote Mère Marie to her son, "that she would have died of regret, if she had been separated from her troupe of little savages."

One little savage had a strange history, and her tale is told, a few words at a time, in letters and in the *Relations*. Her name was Thérèse, and she was brought to the convent by her uncle, Joseph Chihwatenhwa, a baptized Huron who had been in his day a fire dancer, a fire handler, and a medicine man of repute. His peculiar gifts, which came under the general head of sorcery, had been rendered useless by conversion; but, like many another reformed character, he delighted in talking about his unregenerate days. He could, it is said, pick up red-hot stones, put them in his mouth, and thrust his arm into the flames; but he could do none of these things until he had worked himself into a frenzy by dancing and singing. He assured the priests that, far from feeling pain, the contact with fire was refreshing to his hands and tongue.

As for his reputation as a medicine man, that was not difficult to achieve. Père Paul Ragueneau, who was for years the head of the Huron missions, tells us that these Indians recognized

three kinds of illness: natural maladies, super-
natural maladies, and maladies of the spirit.
Natural maladies—the results of overeating, for
example—were left for Nature to cure. Super-
natural maladies were the work of inimical sor-
cerers, and the good offices of the medicine
man were needed to expel from the patient's
body the cause of irritation. Maladies of the
spirit (in other words suppressed desires) were
occasioned by the sick savage's unconscious
need of some object which the medicine man—
having found out what it was—must endeavor
to supply. This sounds like a difficult job; but
it was made easier by an established custom
which held the patient to be cured when the
medicine man said he *was* cured. He might die
a few hours or a few weeks later (just as he may
die to-day after a successful operation); but for
the time being he was healed. To a really clever
person like Joseph Chihwatenhwa the situation
presented no difficulties.

The niece of this accomplished practitioner
became, as might have been expected, an alert
and docile pupil. Her name is mentioned now and
then in Mère Marie's letters, and always with a
word of praise. She was one of the little girls
who wanted to be a hermit. She learned to speak

French, and to sew neatly. She was gentle in manner and speech. After two years in the convent her parents sent for her, and Uncle Joseph was commissioned to take her home. The child was reluctant to go, and the nuns were equally reluctant to send her so far away; but every possible precaution was taken to insure her safety. A fleet of Huron canoes was leaving Quebec. Père Isaac Jogues, who had been collecting supplies for his mission to the Chippewas, accompanied it, and with him went two French *donnés*, René Goupil and Guillaume Couture. Thérèse, sad and silent, was put under their care. Her quiescence was the customary immobility of her race.

From Three Rivers she wrote her first and last letter to Mère Marie, a painstaking little letter which said in schoolgirl fashion, "thank you" and "farewell." Thirty-one miles above Three Rivers the Hurons were attacked by a body of Iroquois two hundred and fifty strong. Some were killed, many were captured, among them Uncle Joseph, Thérèse, and a young cousin, a boy of seventeen. The *donnés* might have escaped, but they would not leave Père Jogues. The prisoners and the captured supplies—a rich booty—were hurried far away, for Montmagny

was at Fort Richelieu, and the savages feared
pursuit.

What followed is the old sickening story of
long-drawn cruelty. It is told in detail in the
Relations and by Parkman. Most of the Hurons,
including their leader, Eustache, were burned,
or tortured to death. Uncle Joseph, who had as
many lives as a cat, Thérèse, and the young
cousin were set aside for ransom or adoption.
The surgeon, Goupil, was beaten, cut, hacked,
and finally brained by an Iroquois. Couture bore
hours of torture with such undaunted courage
that his admiring tormentors adopted him then
and there into the tribe, and never in three years
relaxed their respect for him. Père Jogues was
thought too valuable to be wasted on an eve-
ning's entertainment. The French might ransom
him, the Dutch at Fort Orange had already offered to do so. Nevertheless, he was hated for
his nationality and for his priesthood. The
thrifty savages considered that in his case they
might perhaps eat their cake and have it; they
might torture him first, and sell what was left
of him afterwards.

In pursuance of this plan they cut off one of
his thumbs, crushed and mangled his two fore-
fingers, forced him to run the gauntlet, and

burned his wounded body with lighted torches. When he had partially recovered, the Dutch, with whom the Iroquois were on excellent terms, effected his release, dressed his hurts, and shipped him to Falmouth, whence he made his way to France.

These were the sights which the child, Thérèse, witnessed in her captivity. No harm was done her; but sorrow and pity and fear were her daily portion. Uncle Joseph, that man of many wiles, escaped, and, in the course of time, revisited Quebec. He told the Ursulines, who were full of anxiety about their former pupil, that Thérèse had borne the hardships of her new life bravely and composedly, only saying now and then with a touch of artless self-pity: "The nuns would be sorry for me if they could see me now"; or: "What would they think at school if they knew where I was, or what cruel people kept me here?" In answer to their eager questions he assured them that his niece said her prayers piously. Her rosary had been lost, but she numbered her *Ave Marias* on her fingers, or gathered a handful of stones, and dropped them one by one to insure a proper count. He said also that she was allowed her liberty, and that several young braves had indicated their readiness to marry her. This news was most unwelcome to Mère Marie, who saw in it the undoing of her two years' labor.

Then followed a period in which tidings came brokenly and at ever-lengthening intervals. A far-traveled trader had heard of a Huron girl who lived unmolested among the Iroquois. A wandering Montagnais had seen her with a party of Indians who were fishing. There was a vague rumor of marriage, and then a blank until a transient peace was patched up in 1645. It might have been a lasting peace (I mean by that a peace counted by years instead of months) had Montmagny been of a less confiding disposition. He had shown tact and wisdom in bringing it about. He had persuaded the Algonquins of Sillery to spare the lives of two Iroquois captives, and hold them as hostages, while he despatched a third with messages of conciliation. Guillaume Couture, who had lived for three years among the Indians, helped materially as a negotiator. The Ursulines used their influence so well that one of the conditions made by the French was the return of "a Huron girl named Thérèse to her people."

There is no doubt that the fear and horror entertained for the Iroquois were enhanced by

their occasional—for it was only occasional—
cannibalism. To the reasoning mind, being eaten
after death is nothing like so bad as being tortured before; but mankind at large does not
reason. Marco Polo, who was highly civilized
but not at all squeamish, pronounced cannibalism to be "an evil and a parlous custom," and
the world has so considered it. The fact that
other tribes were not sinless in this regard
(Parkman says that among the Miamis there
was a clan or family whose hereditary duty or
privilege it was to devour the bodies of prisoners burned to death) did not lessen the abhor-
rence felt for the great offender. It is one thing
to be aware of a practice and another to come
into contact with it. "The Iroquois are not men,
they are wolves," sobbed the Algonquin women
who told Père Jacques Buteux how they had
seen their babies roasted and eaten; and the
missionary, who was himself killed ten years
later by the same relentless foe, wrote in the
Relations: "They eat men with more pleasure
and a better appetite than hunters eat a boar or
a stag."

If it be hard to read details of cruelty practised
nearly three hundred years ago, what must it
have been to hear of them as they happened, to

have known and loved the victims of yesterday, to have waited trembling for the tidings of to-morrow, to have gone about one's daily work with this shadow darkening life? Again and again Mère Marie voices her excessive grief at the calamities that have overtaken the Huron missions. New France is no longer "*cette bien-heureuse terre*," but a land of suffering. She implores the prayers of far-off friends, safe by their own firesides. She tells of many deaths, of an occasional escape, of the amazing endurance of fugitives fleeing through the forests without food or shelter. Her soul that had "floated in a deluge of peace" was racked by pity and pain. A strong body of Iroquois ventured to attack Montreal, and were repulsed with loss. They captured and carried away with them a French woman whom they tortured appallingly, wreaking upon this helpless creature their rage and shame at defeat. "Life is a little thing," wrote Mère Marie, "but cruelty and torment are great and horrible realities. Pray, pray, lest our spirits be enfeebled, and despondency deepens into despair."

The Jesuits strove hard to prevent the torture of Iroquois captives who were few and far between. Sometimes they were successful, some-times they failed, hatred being stronger than grace. The Hurons protested stoutly against the baptism of an Iroquois warrior who was to be burned at the stake. They said they did not want their enemies to go to Heaven, they wanted them to go to Hell. It was a mental attitude closely resembling that of the mediæval tribunals which sentenced malefactors to die "without benefit of clergy"; and that of the British judge in India who hanged an offender with a pigskin round his neck, meaning that he should believe himself defiled for eternity. Centuries, races, civilizations, creeds—they may change the face of the earth; but humanity, forever repeating itself, defies them all.

It is but fair to the Indians to say that they believed in their Heaven and Hell as simply and sincerely as if they had been living in the Middle Ages. They were not seeking to play upon a fear they did not share. Mère Marie, writing to an Ursuline nun in France, gives her an animated account of a converted Huron named Charles who delighted in preaching, and who came to the convent to tell his good friends how well he preached. "Do you know what I have done?" he said. "I have been to the villages, and I have instructed young and old, big and little, men, women, and children. I said to them: 'Quit your foolishness! It would be all very well if you had made yourselves, or if you were going to live always in this world; but there is a God, a great Spirit, who has made the heavens and the earth, and everything which they contain. There are two roads, and you must choose between them. One leads you to Hell and the devils; the other to Heaven where He who has made all things lives. If you believe in Him you will go to Him when you die. If you do not believe in Him, you will go down into fire, and you will never get out.'"

"If the love of God does not animate thee," wrote À Kempis, "then it is well that the fear of Hell should restrain thee." Charles was determined to make sure.

The flimsy pretense of peace was rent apart by the Mohawks in 1646. They signalized their change of heart by butchering Père Jogues who had returned to New France as soon as his wounds were healed, and he had received from the Pope a dispensation to celebrate Mass—a privilege from which his maimed hands would have ordinarily debarred him. Père Jérôme Lalemant, the head of the Canadian missions, wrote sorrowfully to Paris that the perfidy of these savages had blasted their hopes of security; but, in truth, nothing had been secure since the governor, putting faith in wampum instead of in guns, had withdrawn the French soldiers from the Huron country. Terrible tidings poured into Quebec. The destruction of the mission of St. Joseph near Three Rivers, and the death of Père Antoine Daniel at the door of his chapel where he had been saying his morning Mass. The destruction of the Petun mission of St. Jean, and the death of Père Charles Garnier, a holy and heroic man who had given up wealth, station, and the charm of life for the martyrdom of a Canadian missionary. His assistant, Père Noël Chabanel, had been recalled from St. Jean; but was surprised and murdered in the woods, as was also Père Léonard Garreau, returning to that "Castle Dangerous," Montreal.

The climax of horror was reached in the deaths of Père Jean de Brébeuf and Père Gabriel Lalemant at St. Ignace. This is the darkest page in the history of New France, and few there are who care to turn it. Père Brébeuf came of a noble Norman family, sharing his lineage (so says Parkman) with the English earls of Arundel. He was tall of stature, strong of limb, stern of purpose, and stout of heart. Père Lalemant was frail physically, gentle in spirit, devout and steadfast. The two priests were singled out for the utmost display of cruelty of which the Iroquois were capable. The details of their deaths are told in the *Relations*, and were read with shuddering dismay throughout France, the bald simplicity of the narrative serving only to heighten its dreadfulness.

It cannot be read to-day. Suffice it to say that Père Brébeuf lived four hours under the torture, and Père Lalemant—incredible as it sounds—seventeen. Père Brébeuf's courage was resolute and unfaltering, a proud scorn of his tormentors mingling with and humanizing the holy courage of the martyr. No Iroquois was ever more defiant of pain; and the savages, recognizing the one quality that they respected, drank his blood and devoured his heart, that the splendor of his spirit might reinforce their own stoicism. Père Lalemant prayed earnestly as long as he had strength for prayer; but long before he died there was left in him no consciousness save that of suffering. He had passed the utmost bounds of endurance, and his dim brain could register nothing but pain. The mangled bodies were found by a party of seven Frenchmen who were sent from Ste. Marie to St. Ignace after the departure of the Iroquois. They heard later from Huron

captives, who had escaped during the journey
through the woods, every particular of the prolonged torture. Christophe Regnaut, a *donné*,
wrote the account for the *Relations*, telling it
precisely as it had been told to him, and winding
up with these simple words: "It is not a doctor
of the Sorbonne who has composed this letter,
as you can easily see. It is a man who has lived
more than he has thought." The skull of Père
Brébeuf, enclosed in a silver reliquary sent from
France, is preserved in the Hôtel Dieu in Quebec,
and his name has passed into a synonym for
valor.

The last victim of this desolating contest was
Père Jacques Buteux, a native of Picardie. His
case is an interesting one because he had long
been considered as too infirm for the Canadian
mission, and had given up all hope of going. Perhaps his superiors thought that a good mentality
and great fervor might outweigh physical weakness. Perhaps the likelihood of a violent death
made health seem of little account. At all events
Père Buteux was dispatched to Quebec; and
at the end of a year Père Le Jeune expressed
some bewilderment as to what had become
of his infirmities. Either cold and a meagre
diet agreed with him, or else he had not the

time to be ill. His tiny chapel was built on a low hill some distance from Sillery. "I have repeatedly seen him," wrote Père Le Jeune, "when the wind had extinguished his lantern, overturned him in four feet of snow, and rolled him from the top of the hill to the bottom. This may well astonish those who knew him in France."

From Sillery Père Buteux was sent to Tadoussac, and thence to Three Rivers. The Atticamegues, or White Fish Indians, who lived many miles northward, begged him to visit their villages. In the early spring of 1651 he made the astonishing journey on snowshoes, and survived it. Those who are curious to know how this could have been accomplished may read his journal published in the *Relations*. It is a fragmentary narrative, but as good as anything of its kind that has ever been given to the world. The following year this dauntless adventurer undertook to repeat his experience. The season was far advanced, the snows were melting, the streams swollen, game was scarce, and every step of the way was beset by difficulties. On the 10th of May the priest, a Huron guide, and a *coureur de bois* were fired upon by a small body of ambushed Iroquois. The two Frenchmen were killed, and their naked bodies flung into the river. The Indian, easily captured because he was carrying a light canoe, made his escape in the forest, and brought back the sorrowful news to Three Rivers.

Throughout these years of warfare, fugitives had poured into Quebec as their only refuge. It had been terribly hard to find them shelter and food; but unstinted charity accomplished this daily marvel. The colonists had very little, but they parted with everything they could spare, and with much that they could not. The Ursulines stripped their convent bare; and Mère Marie, who had mastered the Algonquin and Montagnais tongues, began the study of Huron that she might come into closer contact with the savages who thronged to the convent for food.

When the skies were darkest and hope burned low, when the ranks of the Jesuits were thinning fast, and the ranks of the blessed martyrs were expanding unduly, when Mère Marie's letters had become a repetition of disastrous news, there arrived tidings too good to be credited. The Onondagans, bravest of the five Iroquois nations, had made conciliatory overtures to the unsubdued little colony of Montreal, which had never ceased to put its trust in God, and keep its powder dry. "Naked and defenseless," a delegation of Onondagan warriors confided in the white man's promise, placed themselves in the white man's power, and proudly asked for peace. The French, uncertain whether this was a new and daring ruse or a miracle from Heaven, received their visitors courteously, and watched them apprehensively. Terms were discussed and word was carried to Quebec. "One day," wrote the astounded Père le Mercier, "the Iroquois are burning and killing, the next they are making visits and sending gifts. Undoubtedly they have their designs. God, too, has His."

Chapter VIII

A NEW START

ON THE night of December 30, 1650, the Ursuline convent, "the fairest ornament of the colony," burned to the ground. Snow lay deep on the frozen earth, the icy air held the profound stillness of winter. Suddenly Mère Anne des Séraphins, who had charge of one of the dormitories, started from her sleep to find the room full of smoke, and the flames already licking the floor. Quickly she gave the alarm. There were then in the building fifteen choir and lay sisters, Mme. de la Peltrie, who had taken up her abode in the convent shortly after her return from Montreal, a dozen or so of little French girls, and two score little Indians. All these children were led, carried, or driven into safety; but no time was given them to dress. The fire was sweeping the lower story, and it was hard work herding them to the doors. They shivered in their night clothes, "*toutes leurs robes et leurs petites équipages ayant été brûlés.*" The nuns were not much better off, though some of them had snatched up their cloaks as they fled. Mme. de la Peltrie made her

128

escape in her night dress—"quite an old worn night dress," observed Mère Marie with regret. She evidently considered that a new one would have been more appropriate to the situation.

There was no hope of saving the house, and no time was wasted trying to do so. The good people of Quebec swarmed to the rescue with all the clothing they could carry for the half-frozen fugitives. Mère Marie was the last to leave the burning convent. She had hoped to save some bales of cloth which lay in the vestry, and which would have meant so much to the denuded community, but the flames barred her way. She did, however, collect a few important papers and what money she had before hurrying to the chapel, which was the last part of the building to go. Père Vimont and two other priests had arrived. The blessed Sacrament, the sacred vessels, and a few vestments were carried out. Then the fire took this last refuge and laid it in ruins.

When there was time to ask questions, the source of the catastrophe was quickly revealed. The kitchen and the cook were to blame. "One of our good sisters," wrote Mère Marie to her son, "having to bake the next day, had put her dough to rise; and because the cold was so intense she placed a pan of embers under the bread-trough to keep its contents warm. She meant, of course, to remove this before she went to bed; but, tired and sleepy, she forgot. Another sister passed through the kitchen at eight o'clock, and noticed nothing wrong. As the wood grew dry in the heat it caught fire, and the flames spread unchecked from the bench to the floor, to the walls, and to the room above where Mère Anne des Séraphins slept with the savage children."

No word of reproach for the erring lay sister was ever heard. Mère Marie rivaled Sir Isaac Newton in her forbearance. She could not say with him: "Oh, Diamond, Diamond, you little know what mischief you have wrought" (words no less famous for being apocryphal), because the unhappy culprit knew too well what mischief she had wrought, and her self-reproach needed no augmentation. Nevertheless, to abstain from upbraiding is to insure composure of spirit and a mannerly atmosphere. It was a Roman philosopher who said: "Those who love God bear lightly whatsoever befalleth them," and it was a French nun who proved his words.

If the destitution was complete, the relief was immediate and energetic. "We are reduced to the nakedness of Job," wrote Mère Marie, "but with one great difference. Our friends are compassionate and helpful, which is more than can be said of his." The governor (M. d'Aillebout had succeeded Montmagny) proposed sheltering the homeless Ursulines in the fort; but the hospital at Sillery opened its doors to them, and they gladly took refuge there until Mme. de la Peltrie's house could be prepared for their reception. Mère Marie assured her son that the kind nursing sisters were more troubled about the condition of their guests than were the guests themselves. "They have clothed us with their own gray habits, and have furnished us with linen and with all other necessities. They have done this eagerly and cordially, which was generous on their part for we did need so much. We live as they do, eating at the same table and keeping the same rules" (wise Mère Marie!), "just as if we were of their order."

Three weeks the Ursulines stayed at the hospital, and then transferred themselves to Mme. de la Peltrie's little home which had so fortunately escaped the flames; but which, having been built for two, was somewhat inadequate for sixteen. They knew they would have to remain there for many months, so took their measures accordingly, compressing themselves into the smallest possible space by day, and sleeping in tiers at night. Mère Marie admits from time to time that they are pressed for room; but she has a great deal more to say about the kindness of their neighbors. The Jesuits sent them provisions, linen, bed covers, and all the black stuff held in reserve for new cassocks, so that they might make themselves habits, and return the borrowed gray ones to the hospital. The governor and Mme. d'Aillebout were generous, and everybody lent a helping hand. "No one is so poor that he has not something to offer," wrote Mère Marie. "Every day we receive gifts; a stove, a cloak, a towel, a newly stitched chemise, a few eggs. You know what the country is like, but its charity is greater than its poverty, and Heaven helps us all."

Nevertheless, the prospect of rebuilding might well have daunted the stoutest heart in Christendom. Mère Marie had begged with some show of assurance for her first convent; but how could she approach her former benefactors with demands for a second? She might forgive the heedless sister who left a pan of embers under a wooden bread-trough; but her correspondents in France would naturally think that when they had given money to build a school, it was as little as the nuns could do to keep it standing. Yet it had to be replaced and replaced at once; the need was urgent. The Jesuits, who are always rich because they are always poor, offered to lend eight thousand livres; the governor advanced eight thousand more; and with this sum in hand, Mère Marie, a woman of fifty, whose life had known no respite from toil and care and responsibility, set herself to rebuild a structure which, with its furnishing, had cost sixty thousand livres. "We must do this or return to France," she wrote, "and our courage has not yet fallen so low as to admit defeat. We have not been beaten to the point of flight."

It is needless to say that the Hurons improved the occasion by holding a council, making speeches, and offering the Indian equivalent of resolutions. Naturally they would not lose such a chance. A delegation headed by the chief Taiearoux (whose name uses up all the vowels) proceeded to Sillery, and harangued the Ursulines, Père Ragueneau being present. The oration was sincere, naïve, and touching. "In the fire that consumed your home," said the sachem, "we Hurons beheld again our flaming villages. You are now as poor and as unhappy as we are. Do not leave us. When your friends in France learn that you are houseless, they will say 'Return to your country and your people.' Do not go. Show that your care for us is greater than your love for what is your own. To strengthen your purpose, we present you with two belts of wampum. With the first we beg that you will remain in Quebec, planting your feet firmly on the soil. With the second we beg that you will rebuild your school, and open its doors to our children."

Poor Mère Marie needed no solicitations to remain. Her whole soul cried out against leaving this spot which had seen her hardest labors, her highest hopes, her deepest disappointments. Her feet were, indeed, rooted to the soil, and, happily, land does not burn. Its permanence was to stand her in good stead. Very little of the nine acres had hitherto been put under cultivation; but the convent chaplain, Père Antoine Vignal, a thrifty and resolute cleric, now proposed that every available rod should be turned to account. He took charge of this work in the spring, ploughing and planting as though to the manner born, seeking counsel from farmers, spurring his hired help to harder labour than they had ever known, and raising crops of peas and barley that were the wonder of Quebec. "We have six cows that furnish us with milk and butter," wrote Mère Marie, "and a double team of oxen that serve for farm work, and to draw building materials for the new convent. We can look out of our windows and see it grow. The foundations are laid, the chimneys are in place, in a few days the carpenters will be at work. Pray for me, my dear son, that I may complete the task to which I have pledged my honor and my life."

On the 4th of April, 1653, Mère Saint Joseph, the "laughing nun," died. She came of a noble race, feudal lords in Anjou who had in their day dealt justice (or injustice) with a high hand to their tenantry. She had been sent to the Ursulines of Tours when she was nine years old. There she played, a merry and contented child; there she studied, a gay and popular schoolgirl; and there she was admitted into the novitiate at sixteen. She was twenty-four when Mère Marie asked for her as a fellow worker in Quebec; a wise selection, for the young nun's qualities were precisely those most needed in this field of labor. For some unfathomable reason she is frequently alluded to in the *Relations* as "*cette Amazone*

Canadienne"; but no one could have less resembled those diamond-hard warriors whose
pastime was in battle.

Mère Marie and Mme. de la Peltrie were
women of affairs. They had known the world;
Mère Marie the world of the bourgeoisie, Mme.
de la Peltrie the world of the noblesse. They had
lived, and struggled, and passed through many
vicissitudes. Mère Saint Joseph knew only the
life of a religious. The little savages whom she
tended and taught had no simpler outlook than
hers. She was not a remarkable woman, and she
had no sense of leadership; but for winning confidence, for inspiring affection, for taking life as
it came and extracting savor from it, she was
without a peer in the convent, or in Quebec. The
Indians, young and old, sought her services and
her sympathy. They felt that she, and she alone,
could see clearly the difficulties that beset their
path. It was to her that a baptized Huron, who
had been mocked at by his people, and whom
she exhorted to patience, said simply: "You do
not know how hard it is for a man to be called a
woman."

The poor "laughing nun" suffered sorely in
the last weeks of her illness because of the un-
skillful treatment of the doctors. She was tended

solicitously by Mère Marie, who had brought her to this strange new world, and had laid upon her shoulders the burden now about to be lifted. Night after night the older woman watched by the bedside of the younger, the firelight serving for a lamp. Often Mme. de la Peltrie joined the vigil, or relieved the tired nurse. The savages came daily to ask when they could see their friend, and left uncomforted. They followed her to her grave in the convent ground, and for many months pointed out the spot to trading Hurons, saying simply: "There she lies."

Because of her goodness and the love that was felt for her, stories gathered thickly about Mère Saint Joseph's name. It was said that on the night she died her radiant spirit appeared to an old lay sister of Tours who had taken affectionate care of her when she was a little child. "Dear Sister Elizabeth," the apparition said, "you have a journey to take. Come, come, it is time to start." Smiling, it vanished, and the aged nun wakened, and went to sleep again, confident that her hour was at hand. She died very serenely before the month was out.

Another tale was told of a little French girl, Anne Baillargeon, who had been captured as a child of three or four by the Iroquois, and had been adopted by a woman of the tribe. During the years of her captivity she had lost all remembrance of the white man's speech and of the white man's ways, and had become a hardened little savage, scarcely distinguishable from the Indian children. When the treaty of 1655 brought her release, she naturally did not want to leave the only friends she knew. She fled into the woods, fought fiercely when captured, remained sullen and speechless during the journey to Quebec, and made her last stand for freedom outside the convent door. Enter it she would not, but struggled with her little might to break away and escape. Then came a presence, felt by all, though unseen by any save the frightened, furious child. Silently it took her by the hand. Silently the defiant eyes were raised to meet those other eyes that understood and pitied. Then the snarling lips softened, the tense little body relaxed, and Anne Baillargeon, led by the "laughing nun," turned her back upon savagery, and went with confidence into her new home.

There were now two hopes burning high in Mère Marie's unconquerable soul: the hope of peace restored, the hope of her convent rebuilt. Not for a moment did she entertain the notion that the Iroquois had experienced a change of heart. She understood clearly that when they cried quits with the French, it was because they had another war on their hands (this time it was with the Eries), and preferred concentrating on one foe at a time. Nevertheless, a breathing spell meant much to the harassed and discouraged colonists, who did not themselves err on the side of simplicity. Montreal promised to celebrate with a procession in honor of the Blessed Virgin every anniversary of the blessed day on which had come the overtures of peace; but Maisonneuve permitted no sign of joy or relief to reach the enemy's eye. He held his head high, and his words were few and stern. He asked, as proof of good-will, the release of all French and Indian prisoners, many of whom were, indeed, returned to their homes. It was bitter hard for him to make any terms with savages who had committed such hideous cruelties; but the French were far too weak to dream of subduing their antagonists. That task was left for Frontenac, who thirty-seven years later paid back the long-standing debt with interest.

The Iroquois, on the other hand, laid aside their customary arrogance, and exhibited a truly mystifying suavity. They assumed the open, honest manner that was so endearing in Iago, and expressed a pained surprise that the white man should doubt their sincerity. "My heart is in my tongue," said a warrior to the governor in Quebec, "and my tongue is in my heart. They are one and the same." Père Vimont admitted that he was lost in admiration at the wiles of these accomplished savages. They would make presents of beaver skins and wampum, seeking in return the firearms which they never got. They would profess friendship for the French, and enmity for their allies, the Dutch. They were more than willing to release their captives. "Pray observe the fashion in which they conduct their councils," he wrote in the *Relations*, "and never tell me that they are like brute beasts. *Their education is of the best*. Their purpose is to free themselves from fear of us that they may the more easily massacre our allies. This would be simplified if we would only give them arms. They lack the spirit of truth and honor; but, like the children of this world, they are wise in their generation."

Parkman tells us that the Five Nations, who so successfully terrorized white men and red, never mustered more than four thousand warriors scattered over a huge area. It sounds incredible; for though such numbers seem immense as compared with the numbers of French fighting men, they were small as compared with the massed Indian nations who failed to hold their own against an enemy subtler, bolder, and immeasurably more ferocious than they were. "I had as lief," wrote Père Vimont, "be beset by goblins as by the Iroquois." "Inordinate pride, the lust of blood and of dominion were the mainsprings of their warfare," says Parkman. They were the worst of conquerors; but when conquered, the qualities of their defects induced a savage grandeur which turned defeat to victory. There is an account in the *Relations* of an Iroquois chief tortured to death by the Montagnais, which demonstrates this rather important fact. "I am content," said the victim in the midst of his agony. "You cannot make me tremble or cry. I have slain my enemies, and my friends will slay many more to avenge my death."

There was a note of conviction about the last sentence which must have seriously damped the pleasure of the occasion.

No other American colony ever put as much of its history into print as did New France. The forty-one volumes of the Jesuit *Relations* form but a small part of the literary output. Their especial value lies in their fidelity to facts, and in the closeness of the tie which bound the missionary to his country. He was every whit as loyal to France as to Rome. As a unit of a perfectly systematized whole, his devotion and heroism were tempered by wisdom, and controlled by authority. He and the trader were the only white men who had any real inkling of the Indian's psychology; and, of the two, the priest was the more tolerant observer. "Every mission post became an embassy," writes Mr. William Bennett Munro, "and every Jesuit an ambassador of his race, striving to strengthen the bonds of friendship between the people to whom he went and the people from whom he came. As interpreter in the conduct of negotiations, and in the making of treaties, the missionary was invaluable."

He certainly played an important and difficult rôle in the peacemaking which followed the Onondagan overtures to Montreal. Père Simon le Moyne, who was sent into the heart of the Iroquois country, spent weeks conducting and attending councils, making and hearing speeches, giving and receiving presents; and returned unmolested to Quebec, which was a good deal more than his friends had hoped for. He also had some curious and interesting experiences. One Iroquois chief gave him a New Testament which had belonged to Père Brébeuf, and another a little devotional book which had been found on the body of Père Garnier. Why these relics, so meaningless to savages, had been preserved for several years, it would be hard to say; but Père le Moyne received them as gifts from Heaven. He was shown the salt springs of Onondaga, useless to the Indians who ate no salt, and who believed that an evil spirit dwelt in the waters and fouled them. Game was so abundant, especially on the return voyage, that it seemed to the priest as though the deer pursued the hunters. "My boatmen are in the best humor possible," he wrote in his journal; "for flesh is the paradise of a man of flesh."

Another Jesuit, Père Joseph Antoine Poncet, was instrumental in fixing the terms of peace; but he did not escape unharmed from the hands of the Mohawks. He and a colonist, Mathurin Franchetot, had been taken prisoners at Cap Rouge, and carried into the wilderness; a hard journey made with pitiless speed. When their destination was reached, Franchetot was burned at the stake, and Père Poncet given to a squaw to replace a dead brother. Before disposing of him in this fashion, however, an old Indian examined his hands carefully, called a child of six, gave the urchin a knife, and bade him cut off the captive's left forefinger. The amputation was neatly done, the wound was cauterized with a live ember and bound with a scrap of corn husk, and the priest handed over to his new relative, who treated him with the kindness invariably shown to the adopted. When peace was proposed, Quebec asked for his release, and the Indians deemed him an excellent envoy to carry their terms to the French. It never occurred to them that he owed them a grudge for his lost finger or his lost friend. These things were incidental to war.

Several Mohawk warriors accompanied Père Poncet to Quebec under promise of protection. He came laden with gifts, and so did they. "At last," wrote Père le Mercier to France, "the skies look serene; but the Iroquois are ever and always perfidious. We may think ourselves at peace with them, and find to our cost that they are not at peace with us. They do not, however, seem badly disposed towards the French. Their inextinguishable hatred is for our Indian allies."

The only creature in New France that had profited by the war was the beaver. Freed in some measure from continuous and cruel pursuit, these admirable little beasts had increased and multiplied, and built themselves beautiful homes, and lived in happiness and security. But what was life to them was death to the prosperity of Quebec. "Canada," says Parkman, "lived on the beaver." When the harassed and fleeing Hurons could no longer bring in their yearly quota of skins for exportation, the colonists had no assured income. Père la Richardie says that while the Paris livre was the customary "money of account," the "actual currency" was as a rule the castor or beaver-skin, worth in 1650 about four livres a pound. As the value of the yearly export was often from two hundred thousand to three hundred thousand livres, we can estimate the casualties in the ranks of the beavers, and the money in the pockets of the traders. Now that peace had been temporarily restored, the poor little animals were found to be so numerous that Quebec became almost rich, and Mère Marie, though still weighted with debt, had money to pay the artisans who were putting the finishing touches to her convent.

Such labor as it had represented, such hopes, and fears, and triumphs, and disappointments! Père Le Jeune confessed frankly that he failed to see how the work had ever been accomplished.

He was not without experiences of his own; he had surmounted difficulties in his day; but this structure, bigger and more solid than its predecessor, had gone up step by step in defiance of circumstance. "He who builds here," he wrote, "does not soon come to an end. It is useless to do as did that man who wished to build a tower. *Sedens computabat sumptos suos.* It is useless to reckon principal and income. One is always short in a country like this where everything is twice as dear as in France, and where the few workmen who are to be found do not hire themselves out for a price in silver, but for their weight in gold."

Mère Marie's letters give us a pretty clear insight into the ways and means by which she accomplished her miracle. On the morning of May 19, 1651, the indefatigable Mme. de la Peltrie laid the cornerstone of the new convent; and from that day on every departing ship carried batches of papers, and every ship that came into port brought some measure of help. There was no time to import workmen from France, and Mère Marie considered with Père Le Jeune that wages in Quebec were uncommonly high. "Forty-five to fifty sols [sous] a day to artisans. Thirty sols a day and their food to laborers." She probably got more for her money than did the Jesuit, being trained to business, and having a perilously narrow margin to her account. When it came to providing meals, she no doubt did better than any priest could have done. The capacity of the French middle-class woman to feed her men thriftily and well has been a powerful factor in making France a great and contented nation.

It was uphill work. "Write to me generously," she entreats her son, "and forgive my silence. My family is so big, and I am charged with so many affairs. I must see to it that all we need is sent from France. I must meet all payments for these goods. I must deal personally with the captain of the ship, and persuade the sailors to prompt delivery. There seem at times a thousand little cares plucking me by the sleeve, a thousand things to be remembered and attended to at once." After this exposition of her duties there is something naïve in her remark that she needs the courage of a man to overcome her difficulties. "I feel my way uncertainly step by step, and know not what the future may bring forth."

What it did bring forth was a helping hand in every fresh emergency. There is no denying the skill with which Mère Marie drew into her toils the wealthy and the generous; or else the flame of her spirit communicated itself to theirs. Now and then she paused to marvel at her own success, and to admit that twenty-four thousand livres were "pure Providence." The Jesuits did not fail to set forth her needs in the *Relations*. Père Ragueneau wrote a strong appeal in 1651. Quebec, he said, could not get along without the hospital and the school. They were the things that every stranger asked to see. The colonists were not able to send their little girls to France to be educated; and as for the little Indians, they had no other home, no other chance to be lifted out of savagery, and made into "good Christians and housewives."

It was undoubtedly a trial to Mère Marie that Mme. de la Peltrie should, at this particular juncture, have set her heart upon building a church for the new convent; not a chapel, which was merely a room set apart and dedicated to religious services, but a separate and comparatively expensive structure. It was useless to tell her that the needs of the children came first. She merely replied that it had been the desire of her life to build a church. "God has not given her the grace to detach herself from desires," observed Mère Marie philosophically, and refrained from further comment. It was not

her habit to waste time on arguments. "Avoid
the discussion of grievances," was one of her
axioms; and "Try and get a clearer view of
people with whom we are out of sympathy,"
was another. They help us to understand how
two women so fundamentally unlike as the
disciplined nun and the impetuous *fondatrice*
remained firm friends and co-workers to the end.

With or without Mme. de la Peltrie's help, the
convent was ready for occupancy in the spring
of 1654. On the eve of Pentecost the Ursulines,
escorted by a procession of priests and people,
moved into their new home. Bells were rung and
bonfires were lit. A few months later Mère Marie
wrote happily to her son that, although she was
still in debt, her creditors were kind; and that
the peace had brought a great increase of little
Hurons and Algonquins. She would probably be
compelled to seek new nuns from France. If
only "*ces demi-démons,*" the Iroquois, could
be held off, all would go well. The harvests were
ripening, the beavers were plentiful, the colonists
were full of courage and of hope. Notwithstand-
ing their perils and privations, it was her firm
conviction that they were better off in Canada
than they would have been in France.

Chapter IX

WHITE MEN AND RED

LA HONTAN says that the Canadian farmer lived better than the French gentleman. It is a much quoted statement, but over-emphatic, as are all La Hontan's statements, and written in a period of comparative peace and plenty. Even in Mère Marie's time, however, the grants of seigneuries had begun. The first was ceded in 1623 to Louis Hébert, a Paris apothecary, who came to Quebec when Champlain was governor. A tract of land overlooking the settlement was given to him; and, in the absence of drugs and customers, he turned farmer, felled his trees, built his home, and grew rich in possessions if not in money. The one imperative duty of the seigneur was to induce settlers to come and live on his estate. The ground was rented to them on terms too easy to be burdensome. Six days' labor in the year, a bushel or so of grain, a few chickens or turkeys, a share of the fish caught in the seigneur's river, and the pleasant duty of planting a Maypole before the seigneur's door. Around this Maypole the tenants gathered to gossip and sing; at its foot they built a mighty bonfire in the seigneur's honor, and when that burned low they adjourned to eat and drink under the seigneur's hospitable roof. It sounds, until we look a little deeper into the picture, like the carefree peasantry of the opera.

There is an allusion in one of Mère Marie's letters to the Eve of Saint John, and to the bonfire which was the traditional feature of its celebration; so we know that this ancient custom of France and Germany was preserved in the New World. There was always plenty of wood for the firing. It was the one thing in which the colonists were rich. And if in France, where every little twig is held of value, a town like Amboise can to-day build for Saint John a bonfire so massive and so mighty that it burns twelve hours, what could not Canada with its towering forests accomplish in this regard? These were the pyres on which in the Middle Ages, and long afterwards, were tossed the cats offered as a holocaust to the cruel humor of men. Countless little victims were burned in France before Louis the Thirteenth, then a child, interceded in their behalf, and Henry the Fourth put an end to the sport. Happily the colonists, if not gentle, were certainly not cruel. They were sickened by the prevailing cruelty of the savages, and their natural reaction was to kindness.

It is inevitable that the history of New France, like the history of all other countries, should be written in terms of war. It is not only the frequency of war, but its positive quality and the type of men it creates, which engages our attention. The hostility of the Iroquois had a great deal to do with the character of the French colonist, especially in Montreal where it developed a heroic strain; but if we contemplate it too long the picture is unduly darkened. There was never a time when a large proportion of the farmers failed to sow and reap their crops. They were not safe from Indians, but they were safe from tyrannous laws and harshly administered taxes. Winters were long and summers were short; but the land grew wheat, and rye, and maize, and peas. There was no orchard fruit, but berries were plentiful. Tobacco, that priceless boon, was easily raised. The game, which in France was worth a peasant's life, was free to all who could shoot or trap it. The farmers had stout roofs, hot fires, and rough protecting clothes. What wonder that their numbers increased in spite of the roving strain in the habitant's blood, which brought him to New France in the first place, and which

kept him from settling down when he got there.
He breathed the intoxicating air of liberty, and
t sent him wandering into the forests and over
the waterways; hardy, fearless, quick-witted,
and vigilant, a man who could manage to keep
himself alive when all the forces of Nature con-
spired to kill him. It has never been the habit of
the pioneer to listen too intently for the threat
"which runs through all the winning music of
the world."

Canadian authorities had always to reckon
with the nearness of the wilderness, the lure it
held for men who should have been sober tillers
of the soil, the ease with which these men vanished into its dim recesses. The *coureurs de bois*—
"*coureurs de risques*," La Hontan calls them—
who in the early years had been indispensable
as traders, guides, news carriers, and searchers
for copper, became in time a peril to law and
order. Quebec was comfortable, but the woods
were free, and freedom was the breath of their
nostrils. Farming was profitable, but trading was
more so, especially when pelts were bought with
brandy, and sold privately instead of to agents
of the company. Du Lhut, the most famous of
the *coureurs*, organized his followers into a band,
mapped out their routes, built huts in the forests

for their headquarters, and appraised their wares.
He grew rich if he did not stay rich—preferring
to squander than to save—and he was a hero in
the eyes of the Canadian youth.

Nothing vexed the King more sorely than the
impunity with which these wanderers escaped
from ordinances, and taxes, and tithes, and mat-
rimony, and hard work, and everything that
was decent and admirable in the eyes of sover-
eignty. He ordered laws to be passed, forbidding
unauthorized departure to the woods, and
severely punishing all offenders. These laws
failed to prevent the exodus; but they served to
keep the fugitives in their asylum. Men would
not come back to be whipped and branded and
imprisoned in Quebec, when they might stay
where they were, avoiding with care the hunting
grounds of the Iroquois, having friendly Indians
always within reach, and perhaps an Indian wife
or two if they were domestically inclined. Respectable settlers stood ready to buy their furs,
for the same reason which induced respectable
Englishmen to buy for years smuggled tea and
brandy and tobacco. Louis, ruler of a land where
no outlaw could escape, found it hard to understand conditions in a land where no enterprising
outlaw could be apprehended.

Some controlling and uniting force is essential in every type of community; and in New France, as in New England, this force was centred in the Church. "To the habitant," says Mr. Munro, "the Church was everything; his school, his counsellor, his almsgiver, his newspaper, his philosophy of things present and of things to come. It furnished the one strong, well-disciplined organization in New France." The governors who came between Champlain and Frontenac were not men of penetrating ability. No one of them stands nobly out as does Maisonneuve in the dark setting of Montreal. Parkman says that Montmagny was "half-monk," and D'Aillebout, "insanely pious"; but Montmagny was an adroit negotiator, and D'Aillebout a very brave and able soldier. Jean de Lauzon, appointed in 1651, was a capable man of business, but inefficient as a ruler, and held in some contempt by white men and by red. Argenson was of stronger calibre but his day was a short one; and Dubois d'Avau-gour had the qualities of a commander, when what was wanted was a skillful helmsman to steer in troubled waters.

Nevertheless all these men contributed their share to the well-being of Quebec, which was the social and commercial centre of New France.

The colony was run as sedately as a Puritan settlement, but a wider margin was left for pleasure. Drunkenness and blasphemy were punishable offenses. Church-going was enjoined. But the ascetic Montmagny planted the Maypole at the church door, and bade the soldiers salute it with a volley of musketry. He also provided fireworks for the Feast of Saint Joseph. D'Aillebout was not too "insanely pious" to promote the gayety of New Year's Day; but made a round of visits, and sent acceptable gifts to officials and employees. Even Lauzon laid aside his habitual thrift, and gave gallantly on this most beloved of French feasts. By the time Argenson and D'Avaugour came into office, little luxuries had crept into daily life, little formalities had added dignity to living; and every wedding and christening was made an excuse for entertaining friends and neighbors. The lists of presents, so carefully noted down in the *Relations*, assume a dignified appearance. Pigeon pies and candied lemon peel still hold their own, wax candles are still mentioned with respect, and prunes with appreciation; but cake is coming into notice, capons outrank pigeons, and good French cognac must have warmed many a chilly heart. When we read that the Jesuits sent to the

Ursulines small enameled images of Saint Ignatius and Saint Francis Xavier, to the hospital a number of religious books, and to M. Bourdon, the chief engineer, a telescope and a compass, we know that the day of primitive needs was over.

For a long time after moving into the new convent, Mère Marie's letters are full of hope and of something akin to confidence. She has much to say regarding the excellent deportment of the Iroquois. In the autumn of 1654 she writes that they have returned unharmed to Montreal a young surgeon who had been captured in a skirmish. They have been profuse with promises and presents. They have treated honorably two French *coureurs de bois* whom they had invited to be their guests, and who had temerariously accepted the invitation. They have brought letters from the Dutch colonists at Fort Orange, saying that nothing is so much desired as a truce to hostilities. "It is an admirable thing to hear these savages talk about the blessings of peace," she confides to her son, "for they have chosen chiefs of great repute to be their spokesmen, and all who hear them are impressed with their intelligence."

The French had sought to persuade the Onondagans to send some boys and girls to Quebec as

proofs of confidence and good-will, but in this
they were unsuccessful. Frontenac was the only
governor to whose charge these distrustful—
because perfidious—savages ever committed
their children. But whenever a delegation of Iroquois warriors came for a council, they visited
the Ursuline convent, and expressed their grave
satisfaction with the appearance, the demeanor,
and the accomplishments of the little seminarians.
They asked how long it took to make a French
child out of an Indian child, and they seemed to
have no doubt as to the superiority of the civilized article. Especially were they pleased with
the way the girls sang. We have Père Vimont's
word for it that the savage children could be
taught to sing in such fashion that listening to
them was, if not a pleasure, certainly not a pain.
Their delight in their own performance was so
great that a small child who knew only one hymn,
as *Ave Stella Maris*, would sing it over and over
again for an hour unless someone put a stop to
the diversion.

On one memorable occasion, several Iroquois
chiefs, after listening attentively to half-a-dozen
hymns, offered to entertain in their turn, and
sang strange chants in their own tongue, and to
their own manifest satisfaction. Mère Marie, who

relates the incident, makes no comment beyond an admission that the visitors were "less tuneful" than the seminarians; but to her readers the picture is a strange one. Warriors of the Five Nations laying aside their habitual arrogance, forgetting their native ferocity, and entering into a singing contest with small prim children in a convent school.

There was one Iroquois, however, sterner than his companions, who said a word to Mère Marie which she remembered and took to heart. Her pride in her Indian pupils was natural and commendable, but it was excessive. Père Le Jeune admits that these savage children, wild as little animals when they came to school, fitted themselves quickly into the prescribed order, imitating the French children as best they could, and learning their simple lessons with ease. "If their stability were assured," he adds cautiously, "they would be as civilized as we are." But he remembers the life that lay before them, and has misgivings.

Mère Marie cherished the hope that these docile, intelligent Indian girls would find French husbands. She forgot occasionally that it was to be their mission to carry the seeds of faith into the wilderness, and had a human desire to keep them safe and close in the shelter of a habitant's home. "We have in the school now," she writes, "Huron girls who are as gentle and well-bred as French girls are. They speak French correctly, they dress and behave like their white companions. We believe that in time inter-marriage will become the rule, and this must depend in some measure on the colonists finding Indian wives who can speak their tongue and follow their customs."

With this object in view, Mère Marie spared no pains to make her seminarians sedate, useful, and attractive. From the day that the Ursulines landed in Quebec, and, kneeling, kissed the soil made sacred by the zeal of confessors and the blood of martyrs, they had never wavered in their devotion to work so well fitted to their hands. Père Le Jeune has nothing but praise for the order and discipline of the school, for the precision of method which secured such remarkable results. Even the Iroquois were duly impressed; but one chief observed with disapproval the too manifest pleasure which Mère Marie took in her pupils, her too manifest concern for all they said and did. "You think overmuch of children and of youth," he told her. "All white men do. With us, young people are deemed of little importance. When they speak, no one listens. When they relate marvels, no one believes them. But when warriors speak, we listen and believe. Their minds are firm and hard."

Indian folk-lore confirms this point of view. The child who figures so prominently in the legends and fairy tales of Europe, the youngest son who outwits his brothers, the king's little daughter bewitched by a cruel stepmother, the infant, lost or stolen, befriended by a kindly animal—these familiar variants have no counterparts in Indian traditions. There is only one highly imaginative story of a serpent so monstrous that when it lay coiled around a village of Senecas no man could climb its mighty bulk, and so invulnerable that no weapon could make any mark upon it, yet which was slain by a magic arrow shot by a little boy. We know how mediæval writers would have interpreted this tale; but the Iroquois version stands free of symbolic significance. It is related as a thing of chance.

Most Indian legends are dark with a pervading sense of terror. Not only was Nature a perpetual foe to these poor dwellers on her bosom; but they had managed to acquire that most universal and harmful of all superstitions, a fear of the dead. They feared even the spirits of the animals they killed. They made addresses to the deer, begging them to overlook their slaughter; and they buried the bones of the beavers lest these proud little beasts should resent being devoured by dogs. Père Le Jeune felt and said that the superstitions of the savages were more vivid, and certainly more pardonable, than the superstitions of the colonists who should have known better. The Indian who pounded, burned, and scattered to the winds the bones of an animal that he might dispel the sorcery which threatened his sick friend was more imaginative than an old Frenchwoman—Christian born and bred —who hung around an invalid's neck a bunch of keys as a charm. The stupidity of the thing, no less than its heathenism, offended the fastidious priest.

The Algonquins were especially apprehensive of being haunted by the spirits of the dead. They would try and frighten away a wandering soul by beating loudly on the walls of a cabin; they would spread a net at the door to entangle it; they would burn some stinking herbs or decayed matter to drive it off. Their devices were not unlike the devices by which the Chinese endeavor to keep demons out of their homes; but the Indians never knew the agony of fear which eats out the heart of the Chinese. Their alarm was real, but of a gentler order. What they thought was that the lonely soul wanted to carry with it as a companion to the land of shadows some friend or relative. As no friend or relative desired to go, they took these precautionary measures.

There is one truly terrible story that made part of the folk-lore of the Iroquois. They believed that a nameless monster haunted the forests, and that the bones of the men whom it killed never lay quiet in their graves. Their skeletons were seen swimming with hideous speed and dexterity in the Lake of Teungktoo. Of all the tales of unquiet dead, this is the most appalling. The lonely lake, and the powerful skeletons forever cleaving its dark waters, passing and repassing one another like the damned in the Hall of Eblis.

The temporary peace and comparative plenty which followed the treaty with the Iroquois emboldened Maisonneuve to ask Mère Marie to found a school and orphanage in Montreal. It was in its way a tempting invitation. Labor, hardships, and danger combined to make it desirable from the Ursulines' point of view.

But Mère Marie never lost sight of the feasibility of performance. She would not embark on an undertaking unless she saw some reasonable chance of accomplishing it. Mme. de la Peltrie had made possible the start in Quebec; but there was no *fondatrice* for Montreal, and no money for a foundation. Happily, the children were not untaught, for Marguerite Bourgeoys, a young Frenchwoman who had been an externe in a convent of Troyes, did for them what Jeanne Mance did for the sick and hurt. On her own initiative she opened a humble school in a disused stable, lodged with her little Indians in the loft, and begged the money for their few necessities. Hers was the noblest spirit of the pioneer. The success which crowned her efforts proved their worth. Other schools followed in the wake of her modest venture. She was the good angel of the savages; but she could not give to the French children of Montreal the kind of education which the Ursulines gave to the children of Quebec.

One request, or rather demand, made by the Iroquois envoys was of an amazing and unwelcome character. They sought a French settlement on Lake Onondaga. It was the last thing they had been expected to ask, and the

very last thing which could with reasonable
safety be granted them. It meant a heavy cost
and a much heavier risk. It offered a possible
avenue of trade, and an assured field for the
confessor and the martyr, the one being tolerably
certain to develop into the other. For months
the question was debated; but the Iroquois
pressed hard, and it was difficult to say them
nay. They had certainly treated Père le Moyne
with respect, and with what might have been
termed official affection, calling him father,
brother, uncle, and cousin. "I never before had
so many relatives," he observed. They presented
him with an image of the sun made of six thousand porcelain beads, as a token that the clouds
of misunderstanding had been dispelled by the
rays of friendship which would make even midnight shining and bright. He at least was wholly
in favor of the new mission, and confident of its
success.

So at first was Mère Marie. She writes with
enthusiasm of the devotion of the Jesuits, the
courage and hardihood of the laymen. "The
priests who have been chosen for this venture
deem themselves fortunate. I cannot say with
what zest and fervor they face the countless
hazards of their voyage. Apart from the savages,

who have hitherto shown themselves so ferocious, the dangers and difficulties of traveling in this wild country are greater than anyone in France could ever imagine or understand."

Later on, her growing uneasiness finds expression in a juxtaposition of religious sentiment and political sagacity which has the merit of absolute candor. "Ah, how I long to see a group of Iroquois children in our school," she writes. "How we should cherish them for Christ's sake, and teach them His holy faith. *They would, moreover, be of great service as hostages while our countrymen are in Onondaga.* Not that it would ever be well to consider them as hostages, but only as catechumens. And, indeed, their conversion is the thing we most earnestly desire."

The cost of the venture fell, as was usual, on the Jesuits. Père le Mercier, Père Dablon, Père Chaumont, a French officer, Zachary du Puys, nine soldiers, and a small group of habitants made up the party. They were well received at every stage of their journey; and, on reaching their destination, were charmed by the beauty of the lake, the flocks of wild pigeons, the air of abundance, and the hospitality of their hosts. Feasts were spread, gifts were exchanged, and the Onondagan warriors sang to them by the hour. The sentiments of these bland savages would have done credit to any peace-at-all-price congress in our day. "Farewell war," said one chief, presenting a collar made of seven thousand beads. "Farewell arms. We have been fools till now, but in the future we will be brothers. Truly we will be brothers."

Among the presents offered by the priests was one from the Ursulines, sent as a token that they would gladly receive and teach the Onondagan children; and one from the hospital sisters to indicate that they would be equally ready to receive and nurse the Onondagan sick. These gifts were received with manifestations of delight. "If after this they murder us," wrote Père le Mercier in his journal, "it will be from fickleness, not from premeditated treachery."

In sharp contrast to these diplomatic insincerities was the pathetic joy of the Huron captives at sight of the Jesuits, their only friends. These poor creatures had not been adopted, only enslaved, and their lot was a bitter one. A few weeks after the arrival of the French, a woman of the Cat nation was butchered by order of her mistress, her offense being that she was "too opinionative." She was hacked to death in the open, and the occurrence was so common that it did not even disturb the children at their play

Mère Marie's letters give a more detailed account than do the *Relations* of the perils which beset the Onondagan mission, and of its final collapse. Charlevoix and Francis Parkman take their versions from her. She says that the Jesuits made many converts among the Iroquois. These were mainly women; but the Iroquois women played a far more important part in communal life than did the women of other tribes. They were distinctly "advanced." The French were all housed in one capacious lodge, protected by a palisade. They were tolerably safe from attack; but the savages had a disconcerting custom of bivouacking outside the palisade, and seeing to it that no one left the lodge without their knowledge and consent. As months went by, their manners changed from fervent warmth to sullen civility which carried the shadow of a threat. The trouble, as the priests were well aware, lay with the Mohawks, who had not signed the treaty, and who profited by their independence to raid several Huron villages. This easy and advantageous fighting annoyed the Onondagans who, for all their axioms about peace and trade, were firm believers in the economic value of war. They

wanted their share of the spoils; and their
deepening discontent made them more and
more hostile to the French. Mère Marie is disposed to believe that this growing animosity was
"without doubt the work of demons enraged at
seeing so many souls snatched from their power."
But the Iroquois had no need to be taught by
demons. They could themselves have given a
lesson or two to any imp of Hell.

Happily the French became aware of the plot
for their destruction, and outwitted their hosts.
Secretly they built in the loft over their lodge
two light, flat-bottomed boats to supplement
their canoes. Secretly they laid their plans for
escape. When all was ready they sacrificed their
well-guarded stores and made a feast, a semi-
sacred feast for the savages who gorged themselves to repletion, and slept the lethargic sleep
of the gluttonous. Not one of them stirred when
their prisoner guests embarked at midnight,
breaking the thin crust of ice on the lake, and
paddled swiftly for the Oswego River. It was
reached before dawn; and thirty-four days later
the exhausted fugitives were back in Quebec,
having lost three men who were drowned in the
rapids of the St. Lawrence. It is characteristic
of Mère Marie that she closes her narrative

with a word of pity for the poor Hurons who could never hope to escape, their villages being either destroyed, or lying far beyond their reach. Her friends were safe; they would have been butchered had they remained even a few days longer; she is rejoiced to see their faces once again; but her woman's heart (it was a great heart which could feel and suffer keenly) is wrung with sorrow because Christian Indians, beyond the reach of succor, must live out their lives in slavery.

Chapter X

A PRELATE

RIVALING in bulk the statue of Champlain on the waterfront is the statue of François Xavier de Laval Montmorency, first Bishop of New France, which stands in an open space before the Quebec post office. It bears witness to the part played by this remarkable ecclesiastic in strengthening "the rocky perch of France and of the Faith" which was Champlain's gift to the world. It brings to our minds the vivid picture of a man who fought his way through life; proud, humble, kind, quarrelsome, beloved by friends, begirt by foes, a man apt to be in the right, but incapable of those concessions which hold together a disjointed world, and keep it in running order.

For half a century the Canadian church had been under the nominal jurisdiction of the Archbishop of Rouen who discreetly left it in the hands of the Jesuits. The Récollets had, indeed, been the first in the field, and had done good work; but they were few in number, and lacked the driving force which Saint Ignatius has bequeathed to his sons. When the growing importance of the French colonies, to say nothing of their growing difficulties, called for a spiritual ruler, the Jesuits chose the man. They foresaw, however, many disturbing changes, and so did Mère Marie; for we find her writing to her son, not with the pious pleasure which such an occasion seemed to warrant, but with the apprehensiveness of one well versed in ecclesiastical strife. Things were going well, she said. There was no immediate need for a bishop. The missionaries had done all that mortal men could do. What if someone should be sent who was not of their way of thinking? That she subsequently became an ardent upholder of Laval proves that she had a mind open to doubt and to conviction.

It was not as bishop but as vicar apostolic that the new autocrat came to Quebec. His most noble family of Montmorency stretched back to the days of Clovis, by whose side one of his ancestors had been baptized, assuming then and there the family motto, "*Dieu ayde au premier baron Chrétien*," which was in the nature of a reminder. François Xavier was the third of five sons, and was being educated for the priesthood when his two elder brothers were killed in the battles of Freiburg and Nördlingen. It was then expected that he would lay aside his studies, and take his place as head of the family, his father being dead. This he refused to do, to the distress of his mother who recognized and respected his ability. His rights and titles were transferred to his younger brother, Jean Louis. The fifth son, Henri, entered a Benedictine monastery; the only daughter, a convent. War and the Church took a heavy toll of the great houses of France.

On the 16th of June, 1659, Monseigneur de Laval, titular Bishop of Petræa and Vicar Apostolic of New France, landed in Quebec. A more lovely season could not have been chosen, and the beauty of this sentinel town stirred his heart with a sense of exhilaration and delight. He was honorably received, and the ever-useful house of Mme. de la Peltrie was prepared for his accommodation. It had been made part of the new convent; but the proprieties were observed by building a palisade to divide it from the grounds occupied or cultivated by the nuns. Two hundred livres was the rental paid to its owner, and it was large enough to hold the prelate's modest household. In his suite was a young priest, Henri de Bernières, a nephew of Mme. de la Peltrie's faithful and acquiescent friend,

who, while remaining firmly and safely in France
never forgot the lady in whose service he had
ventured so far. He attended to her affairs,
wrote her sedate letters, and sent her useful gifts.
Mère Marie makes joyous mention of these gifts,
especially of five puncheons (poinçons) of wheaten
flour, a highly esteemed luxury in Quebec where
bread was made of a mixture of wheat, rye,
barley, and occasionally—according to Mère
Marie—ground peas, which gave it a dreadful
density. With the flour M. de Bernières sent a
hundred livres for Mme. de la Peltrie's Indian
children, and that most desirable of colonial
possessions, a clock.

If all classes lived plainly, it was soon apparent that the bishop's conception of plain living fell far below the colonists' comfortable
standard. His austerities were not excessive, but
they were unremitting. They simply meant that
for him the element of pleasure did not enter
into the daily necessity of eating and drinking.
Many of us believe that food was meant to be
enjoyed, and that we are in harmony with the
divine scheme when we enjoy it. This was not
Laval's point of view. His monotonous diet consisted of porridge or broth, dry bread, and a
bit of meat or fish, whichever was forthcoming.

Sweets, even the dried fruit which made the staple luxury of Quebec, never appeared on his table. His drink was hot water flavored with a modicum of wine. His establishment consisted of a house servant and a gardener, the latter being at the disposal of his poorer neighbors. His dress, save when he was on the altar, was threadbare and shabby. He rose early, opened the church doors, rang the church bell, and said the first Mass on the cold, dark winter mornings. "Of all men in the world," wrote Mère Marie, "he is the most austere and the most detached. He gives away everything he has, living meanly and in holy poverty." As he died in his eighty-seventh year, it is plain that his austerities failed to shorten his life. It would sometimes seem as though the body that is hard driven and thinly nourished lasts longer than the body that is pampered with food and warmth and care. Kings are the only men mentioned in history as having died of a "surfeit"; but many a commoner has trodden this ignoble path to the grave.

If the colonists were beguiled into believing that the bareness of Laval's life stood for an excess of humility, they were destined to be rapidly undeceived. A Montmorency was no less a Montmorency for being poorly lodged and badly fed. Laval was a fighter both by nature and by grace; by virtue of the blood which flowed in his veins, and by virtue of the authority he represented. He was as unyielding in small things as in big ones, in matters of precedence as in matters of policy. Should the governor or the vicar apostolic receive the first salute, or be seated first at table? Should the soldiers stand or kneel when they mounted guard at the procession of the Fête Dieu? The poor Jesuits had so much trouble keeping the peace that they may be pardoned for refusing to invite either governor or vicar to their dinner on the feast of Saint François Xavier. It was the easiest way out of their difficulties.

If in matters of no moment Laval refused concession, in matters which concerned the rights and privileges of his office he stood firmer than a rock. It was the age-old dispute between Church and State, the age-old question of what shall be rendered to Cæsar and what shall be rendered to God. Mère Marie, who heard in her convent the echo of discord, appraised the combatants with acumen and with singular detachment. She liked and honored the governor, Argenson, knowing him to be a brave and honest man. She recognized in Laval a higher intelligence, a stronger purpose, a deeper devotion, all the qualities which belong to a maker of history. "Monseigneur our prelate," she wrote to her son, "is zealous and inflexible; zealous in all that appertains to the honor and glory of God, and inflexibly opposed to all that would cast discredit upon them. I have never known any one with a firmer disposition. He will not have a house of his own, but is content to rent a very ordinary one. Yet he stands much on his dignity, and desires all the services of the church to be conducted as splendidly as our simple circumstances can permit. He will do nothing to please those in authority for the sake of support. Perhaps in this regard he may be too stiff-necked; we can accomplish little here without official help. So at least I feel, but possibly I am wrong in saying it. Every one must go his own way to Heaven."

One fertile source of contention was ready to Laval's hand. He found on reaching Quebec a rival claimant to his jurisdiction. The Archbishop of Rouen, who had gradually come to consider New France as an extension of his diocese, had abandoned his policy of non-intervention, and had the year before appointed as vicar general the Abbé de Queylus, a Sulpician priest of Montreal. It was therefore a question of right and might between a vicar general with the backing of the Archbishop of Rouen, and a vicar apostolic with the backing of Mazarin (reluctantly given) and of Rome. In other words, it was a question of whether the Gallican or the ultramontane spirit should prevail in the Canadian colonies.

Both men felt themselves leaders in a just cause. The abbé was a devoted cleric, pious, charitable, rich (the Sulpicians took no vow of poverty), and as autocratic as his opponent, which is saying a great deal. Laval was the stronger man, and had undeniably the higher claim; but Canada was some distance from France, and very far from Rome. As the two ecclesiastics could not well challenge each other, and decide the leadership by force of arms, they were compelled to bide the decision of authorities who were naturally less interested in the matter than were the colonists of Quebec and Montreal. Laval's triumph was assured from the start. The Pope supported the titular Bishop of Petræa, and Louis the Fourteenth put an end to the threatened schism by recalling the abbé to France. There he remained for seven tranquillizing years, until Laval (who in all his belligerent life never cherished any personal ill-will) asked him to return to his labors in Montreal. That he did so humbly and gladly proves him to have had the heart of a missionary, if he lacked the head of a strategist. Montreal was not yet a desirable place of residence.

Laval's quarrels with the successive governors of Quebec were of a more lasting and disastrous character. Argenson had a brother in France who was a counselor of state. To him Laval wrote, complaining of the governor's obstinacy, and to him Argenson wrote, complaining of the vicar's interference. "He thinks he can do what he likes because he is a bishop," said the exasperated official, "and he threatens excommunication." The subjects of dispute were many and varied; but one stood out above all others for forty years—the ever-renewed, ever-agitating question of selling brandy to the Indians. The missionaries had opposed this traffic with all their might since their first coming to Canada; and in Laval they found their most determined and persistent upholder. Under no circumstances would he condone a freedom of commerce which meant the moral destruction of the consumer.

The Indians were the worst drinkers the world

has ever known. They had no use for alcohol except to get drunk on it, and, when drunk, they were invariably quarrelsome and violent. The brandy which was beneficent to the temperate French colonist, warming his cold body and raising his sober spirits, was a deadly peril to the savage. He was like a child playing with fire. Mère Marie, who stood heart and soul with Laval and the Jesuits in this matter, gives us a vivid picture of drunken Indians, even the baptized, sedate, guarded Hurons of Quebec, who became every whit as outrageous as their uncivilized brethren.

"We have a heavier burden to bear than any the Iroquois have laid upon our shoulders. There are Frenchmen so lost to the fear of God that they destroy our converts by giving them brandy in exchange for castors. The consequences are indescribable. Men and young boys grow mad with drink. They run amuck through the streets, shouting, brandishing knives and hatchets, and driving every one in terror from their paths. Murders and monstrous unheard-of brutalities are committed. The reverend fathers have done all they could to check this evil, and Monseigneur our prelate has tried every means within his power to put an end to it. *With his customary gentleness* he endeavored to win over the authorities; but they insisted that the sale of wine and brandy was permitted everywhere like the sale of other commodities. He represented to them that the liberty which was right and reasonable in civilized countries could not be stretched to cover transactions with savages who had to be protected from themselves. Finding argument to be of no more avail than kindness, he was moved by his zeal for religion to excommunicate all who were engaged in such nefarious traffic. Even this thunderbolt failed to ensure submission. The insubordinates claimed that he had lifted into the catalogue of sins against the Church a legal transaction which was not under ecclesiastical control. Now Monseigneur has sailed for France to seek a remedy for such disorders. If he fails, I believe he will never return to Quebec, which would mean an irreparable loss."

He did not fail, and he did return. The intractable Argenson had by this time been replaced by the still more intractable D'Avaugour. Laval obtained D'Avougour's recall, and helped to select his successor, Saffray de Mézy, who made more trouble than either of his predecessors, being a man of equal obstinacy and of less character and discretion. For the time, however, the sale of brandy to the Indians was forbidden, and Mère Marie rejoiced greatly. A permanent measure was not possible for the simple reason that trade was diverted from the French outposts to the Dutch and English which had no handicap. Quebec "lived on the beaver," and the governor was as responsible for the temporal welfare of the colonists as was the vicar apostolic for their spiritual welfare. Consequently the law was imperfectly enforced, and finally repealed when Courcelle and Talon built up the prosperity of New France, and Frontenac sent Joliet and Père Marquette to put the Mississippi on the map of North America.

In 1674 the titular Bishop of Petræa became actual Bishop of Quebec: an appointment which increased his dignity and authority, drew him closer to Rome, and simplified his line of action. If it made him a trifle more unyielding (there was no room for much change in this regard), it gave a fresh impetus to what had become his life's work, the building and maintaining of schools. He was a modern of moderns in his zeal for education, for technical education especially, so far as such a thing was possible in a community of pioneers. His income was inadequate, and was mostly preëmpted by the poor; but the king helped him royally. A seminary for the training of secular priests was his most ambitious project; but attached to it was a "little seminary" for schoolboys whose only instructors heretofore had been the overworked Jesuits. The pupils of the little seminary, both French and Indian, wore by way of uniform a blue cloak confined by a belt. The studiously inclined were taught the humanities, so as to be partially prepared for the priesthood if their inclinations set that way; but by far the greater number were given some manual training to fit them to become artisans. Later on an agricultural school was established at St. Joachim, to teach country lads the principles—as they were then understood—of scientific farming.

All this was in accord with the prevailing spirit of New France. It was not a scholastic spirit. "Canadian children," wrote Abbé de Latour, "have intelligence, memory, and facility. They make good progress; but their instability of character, their dominant taste for liberty, and their hereditary and natural inclination for physical exercise deprive them of perseverance and assiduity. They are satisfied with that measure of knowledge which is required for their occupations. There are few resources, few books, and little emulation."

With the Indians Laval was always on good terms. They offered no opposition to his authority, and he laid the blame for their drunken excesses on the Frenchmen who sold them brandy. This was their own point of view. They had an ingenious fashion of excusing themselves for such misdemeanors by saying that they had not committed them of their own accord. It was the fire water within them which cut, and hacked, and roared, and maltreated children, and shamed the fair name of their tribe. And all against their will.

Laval ransomed Indian captives, baptized the Iroquois chief, Garaktontie, in the cathedral of Quebec, and stood faithfully by Courcelles in his efforts to keep the peace secured by the veteran Marquis de Tracy in his expedition against the Mohawks. "The bishop is a man powerful in word and deed," wrote the appreciative Tracy to Pope Alexander the Seventh. "He is a practising Christian, and the right arm of religion." Indeed these two were firm friends as well as allies. They made a pilgrimage together to the Shrine of St. Anne de Beaupré, enjoyed each other's society, and parted with reluctance when the marquis took his victorious army back to France.

It was a grievous misfortune that Laval and Frontenac, the best governor sent to New France since Champlain, could not keep on good terms. They had many—perhaps too many—qualities in common; and they must both have known that they were so far above the men about them as to be essential to the welfare of the land. That Frontenac preferred the Sulpicians to the Jesuits was no reason for a quarrel. That both men were quick to resent any interference on each other's part was a reason, but not a good one. The wise Colbert in France was infinitely annoyed that so excellent a governor and so excellent a bishop could not work in harmony. The king also was displeased. He spent his life, according to Saint Simon, in adjusting the jealous dissensions of his courtiers, and it seemed to him hard that he should be called on to arbitrate in Quebec.

A divided authority, especially when the line of division can be looked at from different angles, is a prolific source of trouble. When Laval resigned the bishopric in 1688, and retired for a few years to France, his successor, Saint Vallier, took up his quarrels, and added a number of his own. Saint Vallier was a man of irreproach-able life and of superabundant zeal; but there was a hint of John Knox in his discomforting activities. He objected to the extravagance and impropriety of women's dress, which shows that the colonists' wives were beginning to have clothes good enough and gay enough to be no-ticed. When Frontenac proposed that the officers of the garrison should play *Tartuffe*, and as-signed the casting of the parts to Lieutenant Mareul, the new bishop protested so strenuously that the project was abandoned. These cheerful soldiers had already acted with credit Corneille's *Cid* and *Heraclius*, and Racine's *Mithridate;* but Saint Vallier drew the line at Molière.

It was a tempest in a teapot. The Jesuits had always looked with favor, or at least with tol-erance, upon the love of acting which distin-guished the exiled French. Scholars themselves, they had a natural liking for anything that ap-pertained to scholarship. They may also have considered that studying interminable lines of good verse, and reciting them with gentlemanly ease, was as harmless a diversion as Quebec could well afford. The occasional ballets were less to their fancy; but they never interfered, save per-

ıaps in regard to the attendance of very young
people. We know that when the first of these
entertainments was given, eight years after Mère
Marie's coming to Canada, the Ursulines for-
bade the French school children to go to it, and
that one little girl, "*la petite Marsolet*," disobeyed
the injunction and went. A chance allusion in a
letter tells us this much and no more. What
happened to Mlle. Marsolet the next morning is
still a matter of conjecture.

Laval returned to Canada, and lived out his
life in Quebec, the place which in all the world
was nearest to his heart. He spent his last years
in the seminary when it was not being burned
down (which happened twice), or at St. Joachim.
To his young priests he was always a kind and
comprehending friend. The rules he drew up
for their guidance were of a wise and cautious
leniency. Mère Marie praises him as a second
Saint Thomas of Villeneuve. He gave to others
all he had, even his time and strength. When in
1659 a ship brought into port a number of sailors
and immigrants sick of that strange infectious
fever known in English as the "purples" (Ma-
tilda, sister of George the Third and Queen of
Denmark, died of it in Celle), Laval nursed day
and night in the hospital. He was exceedingly

deft in bed making, and in every art that added
to the comfort of his patients. It was useless to
represent to him that his life was too valuable
to be risked in this fashion. He merely replied
that here was work to his hand which he could
do better than most volunteers. Several of the
nursing sisters caught the fever which spread
in a modified form through the town. "Thank
God, our community has escaped," wrote Mère
Marie. "We are in a high and healthy spot, ex-
posed to winds which blow away infection. The
air is clean and cold. We are in excellent condition."

So the years sped by. Laval's popularity and
authority had greatly increased since he resigned
the bishopric. All men revered his single-minded-
ness, his self-denial, his amazing industry, his
deep devotion; qualities that took on a finer
lustre with age. When he spoke, they listened;
when he counseled, they obeyed. The mischiev-
ous and uncivilized custom of charivari, which
had obtained a hold in Quebec, was abandoned
at his solicitation. He lived to see Frontenac
recalled to France, and the disasters which
brought him back as the sole hope of the imperiled colonists. He lived to see the massacre
of La Chine which Frontenac amply avenged;

and the invasion of the English under Sir William Phipps, an invasion which his young farmers of St. Joachim, like the "embattled farmers" of Concord, helped stoutly to repel. When the ship on which Saint Vallier was returning to Quebec fell into the hands of the English, and the bishop was detained in London for five years, Laval "carried on" in his absence with renewed energy, and possibly some enjoyment of the situation. Age seemed powerless to affect him. "My health is exceedingly good," he wrote, "considering the bad use I make of it." He took the hard journey to Montreal to administer confirmation when he was seventy-nine. He sang the High Mass on Easter Sunday in the cathedral of Quebec when he was eighty-four. He died at eighty-six, and the watchers by his bedside asked for a few words of exhortation, such as many holy men have uttered with their last breath. Not so Laval. "They were saints," he said sternly. "I am a sinner." And with these noble words upon his lips, his soul spurred to the judgment seat.

Quebec holds his memory dear, and his spirit dwells in Laval University, the big descendant of his small foundation. Its spacious and agreeable shabbiness, so unlike the wealth-laden uni-

versities of our wealth-laden land, reflects faithfully the image of the austere and dauntless
pioneer priest, the supremely human laborer in
the vineyard, who felt himself to be a sinner,
but who did work enough for half-a-dozen saints.
There is a sentence of René Viviani's which gives
us with singular lucidity (such are the haphaz-
ards of inspiration) a clue to this life force: "No
man can say that he draws strength from himself alone. Heart and soul and mind and body
would break were he to try it." Heart and soul
and mind and body held together unbroken
through Laval's eighty-six years. He drew
strength from the faith that was in him.

Chapter XI

"DANGER'S TROUBLED NIGHT"

By 1660 the colonists had ceased hoping for peace. Their training and experience had not fitted them to live in a fool's paradise; but rather to recognize every sign of danger, and to be perpetually on their guard. The Mohawks were openly hostile; but the other Iroquois nations were playing a more dangerous because more subtle game, covering up bad deeds with fair words, weakening the outposts of French civilization that they might more securely attack its strongholds. Every year their depredations increased, their urbanity diminished. In a daring raid on the Isle d'Orléans, Lauzon's son was killed, and the body horribly mutilated. Mme. Picquart and her four little children were captured at St. Anne. That Quebec was saved from assault was due primarily to information given by a warrior of the Mohegan or Wolf tribe who had been adopted as a child by the Iroquois, and who was taken prisoner and burned by the Algonquins. This unfortunate consented to be baptized, and "told all he knew"—to quote the words of Mère Marie—before being bound to the stake. He said that eight hundred Iroquois had planned to attack the French, and were even then on their way; but of their immediate whereabouts he could, or would, say nothing.

Argenson's faith in the Mohegan's report prompted him to take immediate action. The defenses were strengthened, the streets were barricaded. The nursing sisters and the Ursulines were removed to the new Jesuit buildings; the first because the hospital was in a perilous position, the second because the school, high perched and strongly built, was occupied by troops. Mère Marie was extremely reluctant to leave her spotless and neatly furnished convent to the rude handling of soldiers. She asked permission to remain, and, with the wisdom of the serpent, backed her request by offering to feed and serve the garrison, keeping with her for this purpose three lay sisters. The offer was too tempting to be refused. The four nuns worked so hard all day, and were so tired by night, that they had no time to think about the Iroquois, and the men were probably better fed than they had ever been in their lives. Mère Marie was, however, much impressed by the thoroughness of Argenson's preparations:

"Redoubts were built," she wrote to her son, "the strongest being near our stable. It defended the church on one side, and the barn on the other. All our windows were boarded and pierced with loop-holes. The only means of exit left in the court was one little door, barely wide enough to permit a single man to pass through it. In a word, our convent was turned into a fort, garrisoned by twenty-four brave soldiers. The whole town was safeguarded. The approaches were patrolled day and night. A dozen great dogs helped to keep watch and ward."

And where were the Iroquois so fearfully apprehended, so slow to materialize? The eight hundred may be considered as a figment of the Mohegan's brain. He had told more than he knew; and if he took a saturnine delight in frightening his captors, who can begrudge him this final satisfaction? Nevertheless there were savages prepared for war and advancing to attack. The danger, though not overwhelming, was acute. It was averted by one of those dauntless deeds which would seem beyond belief were it not for the ineradicable heroism of men's hearts.

A young Frenchman of Montreal, Adam Daulac, Sieur des Ormeaux, had heard the Mohegan's story. He was twenty-five years of age, strong, fearless, resolute, and weary of waiting for an evil day. Therefore he asked for a handful of volunteers to carry the war into the Iroquois country. He did not propose to accomplish the impossible; but he knew just how much might be done, and he stood ready to do it. Sixteen men of varying occupations, and all, like their leader, young, offered their services—in other words, their lives. Maisonneuve consented to their departure, and perhaps, bearing always on his shoulders the intolerable burden of danger and responsibility, envied them their brief adventure and their certain death. It was not for them a question of returning with their shields, or on their shields. They would do neither. The wilderness would receive their broken bodies, and their faces and their names would be forgotten. They confessed, communicated, and at the foot of the altar swore an oath that they would accept no quarter. Four Algonquin warriors and a small body of Hurons joined them. Scantily equipped save for arms and ammunition, of which they carried as much as their canoes could hold, they bade farewell to Montreal, and started on their long and last journey.

Great numbers of Iroquois had wintered in

the woods that bordered on the Ottawa, and it was Daulac's audacious design to waylay them as they descended the river. He and his men entrenched themselves behind a rude but strongly fashioned palisade at the foot of the rapids known as the Sault St. Louis. When the first canoes filled with Senecas, who thought themselves safe from molestation, came swiftly down the stream, they were greeted by a deadly fire. The unexpectedness of the attack scattered their fleet; and as they naturally wanted to know the strength of the enemy, they asked for a parley which was curtly refused. Daulac had not come all that way to talk.

Then followed five days of the strangest warfare ever seen. A fast-growing horde of Indians held at bay by seventeen Frenchmen behind a barricade that looked even more insignificant than it was. The Hurons, being promised their lives by the Iroquois, who had no intention of keeping the promise, deserted promptly—all save their chief, Annahotaha, who, seeing his own nephew about to fly, shot him dead. The Algonquins, made of sterner stuff, held their ground. The enemy lost so many warriors, including the Seneca chief, that but for the very shame of the thing they would have abandoned the contest. As it was, learning from the Huron deserters the weakness of their opponents, they drew together their forces, made a massed attack, and smashed their way through the flimsy pretense of a fort. Its defenders, mindful of their oath, fought to a finish. Daulac was killed in the first onrush. When the Iroquois took stock of their spoils, they found thirteen Frenchmen, the four Algonquins, and Annahotaha dead. Four Frenchmen were still breathing; but of these, three were so near the end that their captors lost no time in building a pyre, and flinging the dying men to the flames, hoping against hope that they might still have life enough in them for a few minutes of agony. The fourth, whom they judged might possibly live for a time, was reserved for more leisurely handling.

Twenty-two men died on the shores of the Sault, but they did not die in vain. Troubled and humiliated by their losses, the Iroquois had no mind for further fighting. They turned back sullenly, asking themselves what manner of men these were who battled against hopeless odds. A fear, half normal, half superstitious, filled their savage hearts. Courage was good, they were themselves courageous; but it was courage with victory as an end. The Frenchmen could never have dreamed of victory. They had come to the Sault to die.

Escaping Hurons brought back the news to Montreal and to Quebec. It must be said for the Hurons that if they were indifferent fighters, they were adepts in flight. They were the jail breakers of the wilderness. No bonds—and the Iroquois bonds were sternly fashioned—could hold them fast. Pegged down securely at night, they were missing in the morning, and the friendly forests hid them from pursuit. Mère Marie, who tells at inordinate length and with many doubtful details the story of Daulac's adventure, was reluctant to believe that these friendly Indians played so sorry a part. Her informants were Huron fugitives, who were naturally disposed to present themselves in as good a light as was consistent with the fact that they were living, and the French and Algonquins were dead. She clearly understood the nature of the service which had been rendered to New France. Had the Iroquois made their attack that spring, they would have found the defenses— save in Quebec—inadequate, and the farmers scattered in the fields. Now, realizing the certainty of the danger, Argenson redoubled his precautions.

"We know for sure," wrote Mère Marie, "that the savages will return in the autumn or in the following year, and we are making ready to receive them. The governor has compelled every village to build a small fort and a strongly protected communal granary, so that the men can defend themselves and their harvests. He bears always in mind the danger of famine; for if the Indians descend upon us in the spring, they put a stop to the sowing, and if in the autumn, they ravage the crops."

Père Boucher bears witness in the *Relations* to the reverential gratitude which was felt for Daulac and his companions, as for men who had laid down their lives for their friends. "Well may we give glory to these seventeen Frenchmen of Montreal," he writes. "It would be shameless to do otherwise, for it was for us and for our homes they perished. By their deeds and by their deaths they have averted—at least for a time—the storm that threatened to destroy us."

It was never fair weather for long in New France. If the Indians refrained from pernicious activities, Nature took a hand, and saw to it that her sons should not grow soft through safety. Five years lay between the death of Daulac and the final outbreaks which brought the Marquis de Tracy as lieutenant general to Quebec. These years were fairly well filled with savage raids and internal dissensions; but in 1663 the colonists experienced a disturbance of a different order—an earthquake of exceptional and terrifying severity. It came without warning on the 5th of February, the Feast of Saint Agatha. The atmospheric disturbances which often precede such an event were conspicuously absent. There were of course the usual number of persons who (being on the safe side of prophecy) recalled dreams and visions in which they had been distinctly told what was about to happen. There were others who had seen strange signs in the heavens, blazing serpents and balls of fire that scattered sparks like rockets. But as none of these portents and predictions were confided to the public until after the earthquake was over, the colonists were happily spared the terrors of anticipation. There is a good account of what happened in Quebec written by Père Jérôme Lalemant in the *Relations*, and there is a still better one written by Mère Marie in a letter to her son. She had always the gift of narrative:

"The day," she wrote, "was absolutely serene when of a sudden we heard a loud rumbling as if hundreds of carts were rolling with mad speed through the streets. Yet this sound seemed to come at once from the earth and from the air, a strange and terrifying thing. A roaring as of winds and waters was in our ears. A shower of stones came rattling on the roof, as though the rocks on which Quebec is built had been torn from the soil, and tossed down on us from the sky. A thick dust filled the air. Doors opened and shut of their own accord. The church bells clanged, and all the clocks in the convent struck at once. The floors heaved, the walls swayed. Chairs and tables were overturned. Amid the confusion we could hear the barking of dogs and the distressful bellowing of cattle. We ran out of the house and felt the earth tremble under our feet. It was as sickening as though we stood on the unquiet deck of a ship. Men and women flung their arms for protection around the trunks of trees which seemed to give way under their grasp, while the branches sweeping downward struck at them angrily. The terrified savages, possessed by the belief that the souls of the dead were responsible for all this uproar, fired their guns in the air to frighten them away, thus adding to the indescribable tumult and commotion."

The shocks continued with lessening violence

throughout the night. Mère Marie says that some
of the watchers counted thirty-two; but as she
herself was not aware of more than six, we may
be tolerably sure that six was the number. All
night she knelt in the church, the new church
built by Mme. de la Peltrie, and which, though
"small and plain," had cost a great deal of
money. The strong stone houses of Quebec stood
firm, and not a life was lost. But along the banks
of the St. Lawrence heavy landslides changed the
face of the country. The river charged with mud
and ground-up rock was undrinkable for months.
Near Tadoussac, where the shocks were heavy
and continuous, a fair-sized hill crowned with
trees sank into the water as though it had been
a pebble. Springs were dried up, and little
streams turned from their courses. There were
no roads to destroy, but travel was made in-
creasingly difficult. The uneasy earth quieted
slowly; and only when midsummer brought her
peace did she resume her friendly and familiar
aspect, and the fear in men's hearts was stilled.

The area covered by the earthquake was a wide
one. As news came to Quebec, Mère Marie heard
of the deadly peril of Montreal and Three Rivers,
of the plight of Fort Orange, and of the extreme
terror of the Iroquois, whom the Dutch had as-

sured—on the authority of a local prophet—that the world had but three more years to live. Five French captives had been ransomed and sent home by the friendly Hollanders. "They have always been kind to our poor prisoners," wrote Mère Marie gratefully. A British ship came into port, and the sailors told her that in Boston, "a beautiful town which the English colonists have built," the shocks had been very severe, and had lasted five hours and a half. There was little news that failed to find its way to that fenced-in convent and to those listening nuns.

It was inevitable that the fright experienced by the colonists and their long weeks of suspense should bring about a religious revival. The churches, always full, were now crowded. The indifferent became devout, the devout redoubled their devotions. Mère Marie reported joyously that men were searching their consciences, confessing their sins, and giving thanks for their preservation. "At the same time that God shook the rocks and the mountains of this wild country," she wrote, "He shook the souls of men. The days of careless living have been changed to days of prayer. Processions and pilgrimages succeed one another soberly. Young and old are fasting on bread and water. Priests are spending long hours in the confessional, absolving penitents. Enemies are reconciled. Sinners openly acknowledge their transgressions and promise amendment."

This last statement was especially true. Sinners are always ready to make the most of their opportunities. Mère Marie relates, among other instances, the case of a soldier at Fort St. François Xavier who had led a loose life, and who was so terrified by the first shock that he cried to his companions: "No need to look further for the cause of this catastrophe. I am the sinner whom God punishes for his offences." If this poor fellow exaggerated, after the manner of his kind, his importance in the Divine scheme, he was at least sincere in his conversion, which, we are assured, was permanent.

It was all very natural and very human. If the colonists were fairly inured to danger, it had hitherto been the kind of danger which called for action on their part. When the Iroquois were at their doors, they knew that it was a case of Heaven helping those who helped themselves. But when Nature is in a revolutionary mood, man is subdued to humility. He is, as ever, the captain of his soul; but he is not just then the master of his fate, and he has reasonable doubts of contingencies.

Five years after Daulac's expedition, and two years after the great earthquake, came the Holy War, so called because it was meant to decide, and did decide, the permanence of the French occupancy. Louis the Fourteenth in the heyday of his youth and power never lost sight of New France. He had a sincere desire to advance its interests; and if his measures were sometimes fluctuating and uncertain, this was because of the multiplicity of his counselors. He could not have sent better men than Courcelles and Talon as governor and intendant, and he could not have given them better advice in regard to the friendly Indians than in this often quoted letter of instruction:

"The first desire of the King is to bring about the conversion of the savages to the Christian Catholic faith; and to that end his subjects are enjoined to treat them justly, kindly, and gently. No wrong nor violence is to be done them. Nor is their land to be taken from them on any pretence whatever. *Certainly not because the French colonists would make better tenants of such land.*"

How does this last sentence sound to the ears of Americans familiar with the tragic history of Indian reservations?

If savage allies were to be treated with kindness and consideration, savage enemies—and first and foremost the offending Mohawks—were to be taught a stern lesson; and their chosen instructor was an officer of some renown, Alexandre de Prouville, Marquis de Tracy, lieutenant general in the army of France. He was sent first to the West Indies, and then to Canada, reaching Quebec on the 30th of June, 1665. His landing was a great event in the annals of the colony. He brought with him four companies of the first regiment of regular troops ever sent to New France, and he was furthermore accompanied by a number of well-born young men eager for adventure. The pomp and splendor of his following amazed the habitants. Twenty-four guards and four pages led the way. Richly dressed gentlemen walked by his side. Tracy was sixty-two, heavily built, and consumed by a fever caught in the tropics; but he climbed the steep heights to the fort, and to the cathedral where Mass was said; refused the comfort of a *prie-Dieu*, refused a cushion, and knelt on the rough stone floor until the service was over and

the *Te Deum* sung. Mère Marie reports his edifying conduct, his cordial bearing, his great size,
and the hopes he aroused in men's hearts:

"M. de Tracy has been wise and watchful.
I believe he is a man chosen by God to bring
us order and safety. He bids us remember that
this expedition is in the nature of a holy war.
Père Chaumont goes with him because he speaks
the Huron and the Iroquois tongues like an
Indian born. Père Albanel and other priests will
interpret the Algonquin and the Montagnais.
We all know that unless we can defeat and hu-
miliate the hostile savages, they will eventually
drive us from the land."

The Mohawks, whose outrages had grown in
frequency and ferocity, were to be attacked in
their strongholds, a thing which had never been
dared since the first colonists had come to New
France. The invasion was planned on a scale
which for the time and place seems heroic. The
regiment of Carignan-Salières arrived in de-
tachments, Salières, its colonel, landing with the
last companies. All was in readiness; but, before
starting, the wily Tracy built three new forts
at salient points, Fort Richelieu, Fort St. Louis,
and Fort Ste. Thérèse, to protect Quebec from
raids. He took with him six hundred French

soldiers, five hundred Canadians trained to arms, and a hundred and ten "bluecoats" of Montreal, so called from the hooded mantles that they wore. They were the hardiest woodsmen in the country, skilled in the use of snowshoes, well versed in savage warfare, difficult to kill and impossible to daunt. There were also a hundred Indians who served as scouts and runners.

It was a magnificent fighting force; but a bit cumbrous for transportation over a strange and wild country. It could be trusted to subdue the Mohawks if it could get at them; but no marching to and fro over Europe could prepare troops for a Canadian wilderness. Crossing Lake Champlain in three hundred large canoes was easy work; crossing Lake George was not much harder; but then came a mountainous march of a hundred miles with an Indian trail by way of road, and with every obstacle that Nature could devise to bar their progress. The difficulty of transporting provisions was very great, and white men, unlike red men, could not do without food. Every member of the party, officer as well as private, carried his own belongings, and this was no easy matter for the unaccustomed. Père Chaumont confessed later to Mère Marie that the burden on his back rubbed it sore, and gave him a painful tumor. Fortunately the season was October, and streams, which in the spring-time would have been drowning deep, were easily forded. Also the chestnuts were ripe, and kept the hungry troops from semi-starvation.

On the 15th of October, being the Feast of Saint Theresa, the first Mohawk town was sighted. A heavy storm promised the possibility of a surprise, and Tracy pushed on all night through the soaked and dripping forest. When he emerged in the morning there lay before him a compact, stoutly constructed, well-protected, empty village. A few Indians perched on surrounding rocks fired aimlessly. The rest had retreated to a higher stronghold. The Frenchmen were tired, wet, and hungry, but their leaders knew the danger of delay. A morsel of food, and they followed the trail, this time a broad and well-trodden one, which led to the second village. It was deserted like the first. So were a third and a fourth. In the last, however, they found an Algonquin squaw, long held a captive, who told them that the Mohawks had entrenched themselves behind the walls of Andaraqué, the highest, biggest, and strongest of their towns, to which she joyfully offered to lead them. Dusk was falling when the French made their final assault, and found to their amazement that the triple palisade, twenty feet in height, was undefended. An infirm old Indian, two squaws, and an abandoned little boy were the only inhabitants of Andaraqué. The savages, panic-stricken by the size of the invading army ("the whole world is coming against us!") and by the frenzied beating of the drums, had fled to the inviolable security of the woods.

Yet when Tracy and Salières examined the defenses of the Indian stronghold, they marveled that it should have been so easily surrendered. The Mohawks had learned much from their allies, the Dutch, and this fortified town was apparently prepared for attack. The size and comparative comfort of the lodges, the great stores of food laid up for winter use, the tools and household utensils, the warm furs and gay apparel, all told their tale of savage affluence. The French soldiers took what grain and booty they could carry (one hundred kettles found their way back to Quebec), and set fire to the village. Even the palisades were burnt to the ground. The squaws threw themselves despairingly into their flaming homes. The little boy was carried—with the kettles—to Quebec, where Mère Marie pronounced him a handsome child.

The four other villages were destroyed, and the Mohawks left to face the winter without food, shelter, or equipment:

"God has done for us what He once did for the people of Israel," wrote Mère Marie. "We were victors without a blow. Had the savages, well armed and strongly fortified, stood by their homes, our losses must have been severe."

There were not wanting those who censured Tracy for leaving the Indians unpursued. "With half that number of men," they said, "Maisonneuve would have fought the Mohawks to a finish." But against savages scattered and hiding in their familiar forests, massed troops are at a terrible disadvantage. Tracy, like a good general, saved his men, and let Nature do the work for him. He illustrated Sheridan's cruel pleasantry, spoken two centuries later, concerning the crow which would have to carry its own rations if it flew over the ravaged land. The ethics of war are not affected by time, or race, or circumstance. How many Mohawks perished that winter, nobody ever knew; but their strength was broken, their spirit crushed, their prestige with the Five Nations destroyed. The blow was not a final one; there are few finalities in the world; but for twenty years something resembling peace reigned in the land. New France secured a fresh lease of life. When that expired, it was renewed by Frontenac's hand.

While the Holy War was reaching this satisfactory conclusion, Quebec waited and hoped and prayed. Three weeks after the departure of the troops, Mère Marie wrote to France: "We know nothing of what has befallen. God, who is the God of battle, knows all. If He has aided us, we are victorious. His holy will be done; for in the order of this will He is glorified by our losses no less than by our gains. Nevertheless we are having the forty hours devotion in our four churches, and never cease our prayers. We feel that on the success or failure of this expedition depends the life or death of the French colonies."

When Tracy returned with his good news and his undiminished forces, he was disposed to elude as far as possible the ceremonious congratulations and rejoicings which are the plague of the victorious soldier. He was bulky, he was gouty, he was feverish, he was fatigued, he wanted to be let alone. The sympathetic and grateful French forbore to harass him; but the Indians were not to be gainsaid, and he let them have their will. The Hurons made him six gifts, accompanied by six orations. The Algonquins made him nine gifts, accompanied by nine orations. He could not understand a word that was spoken, save as interpreted by the Jesuits, and he did not want the gifts; but he remembered the king's instructions, and behaved with patient urbanity. When, however, deputations of Iroquois—now thoroughly frightened and keen for peace—arrived with fresh gifts and fresh orations, he grew restive. Especially was he weary of collars and belts of porcelain (wampum), and he asked if he might not refuse them —a suggestion which froze his hearers' blood with horror. It was represented to him that such a deed would shake the foundations of society. Words might be lies, promises might be broken; but wampum was a sacred thing, the symbol of authority, the bond of friendship, the record of treaties, the sign and token of all that the red men valued. To reject it would be an unpardonable and unforgettable insult.

Tracy yielded with a good grace to these arguments, and accepted a fresh supply of beadwork; but he said very plainly in replying to the Iroquois speeches that his master, the great king, desired deeds not words, friendship not gifts. He demanded the return of all captives, and the surrender of hostages as a guarantee of good behavior. That his terms were accepted, and the conditions fulfilled, proves that these arrogant Indians had been for once subdued by the vision of the power of France.

For Mère Marie, Tracy conceived a very deep respect. A man of swift decision and of timely action, he measured her worth by her work. A far-traveled man of the world, he admired her grave composure and direct speech. Before leaving Quebec, he gave her a proof of his regard. When the convent church—Mme. de la Peltrie's church—was being built, and money was running short, Père Jérôme Lalemant demurred at the expense of a little side chapel, some twelve feet square. Mère Marie, who greatly desired this chapel, pleaded that it was included in the plan, and would cost only four hundred livres. Père Lalemant said dryly that four hundred livres would go a long way toward supporting a savage orphan; and Mère Marie, finding this argument irresistible, yielded to it without further words. Ten years later, when Tracy was being shown the convent and the church, one of the nuns said: "This is where our Mother wanted a chapel." Whereupon the gallant commander offered then and there to build one for her; and he did so on such a lavish scale, and with so complete an unconcern about the savage orphans, that it was said to have cost twenty-five hundred livres.

What wonder that Mère Marie, who had the most amazing knack of getting sooner or later what she wanted, wrote enthusiastically of Tracy's goodness and intelligence? What wonder that she regretted his departure for France? "He was the best friend we have ever had in this country."

Chapter XII

THE MARRIAGE MART

"SEND me wives," wrote that gallant adventurer, Pierre le Moyne d'Iberville, when he was exploring Canada's waterways, and building her forts. "With wives I will anchor the roving *coureurs de bois* to the soil of New France, and make of them the farmers that we need."

It was an oft-repeated cry. Talon, who never lost anything through not asking for it, importuned the king so stoutly for both men and women colonists that Colbert told him plainly that his majesty could not depopulate France to people Canada. Soldiers he must have to guard his realm and fight his battles; but, by the same token, there were many marriageable girls to spare, and Quebec should have her share of them. Louis expressed himself as being well pleased that only sixteen of the last boatload of maids should have been left unmarried at the end of a few months.

In truth the whole question of marrying and giving in marriage had been a serious problem from the beginning. There were few white women among the early settlers, and the Indians had been used to easy and frequent divorce. "Ah, but these savage marriages give us trouble," sighed Père Le Jeune. The looseness of the tie appalled the missionaries, and a hard-and-fast bond was inexplicable and unwelcome to the Indian convert. Now and then we catch a note of sympathy for his dilemma on the part of an understanding priest. Père Vimont, for example, expresses something akin to pity for the young brave who is compelled to "bend his neck under the yoke of marriage which may one day lie heavy on him." He plainly considers that to patiently and profitably bear this yoke requires "a miracle of grace." A Frenchman is from first to last a man's man. He cannot be anything else. It is this characteristic which has made the Frenchwoman sane and balanced. She has not disintegrated under adulation.

Mère Marie had always hoped to supply the needed wives by marrying her Huron and Algonquin girls to settlers. The Church favored such unions, but there were not enough pupils to be of much service to the rapidly growing colony, and many of them preferred men of their own race. When they had been taught to read and write, to speak French and wash themselves, to sing hymns and say their rosaries, they carried these accomplishments into the forest, and lived their old savage lives. The ingrained docility which had made them such good school children made them obedient wives. Responsive to surroundings and to control, they relinquished the niceties of civilization as unprotestingly as they had acquired them.

In this regard Mère Marie tells a strange and touching story. When the Iroquois surrendered their prisoners in fulfillment of their promise to Tracy, a number of squaws were sent to Quebec, and placed temporarily under the care of the Ursulines. Among them was an Algonquin girl, who, although a captive and no better than a slave, had been taken to wife by an Iroquois warrior. Indian marriages were, as a rule, practical rather than romantic; but this young brave set so high a store by his woman that he followed her to Quebec, and besought Mère Marie to give her back to him. She told him that she could not release her charge. The governor must do that. She told him that if he wanted the Algonquin as a wife, he must be baptized, as she had been in childhood, and must marry her in Christian fashion. He consented eagerly to both demands. He would do anything, be anything. Only give him the girl. Filled with dread lest her people should carry her away, he haunted the convent, pleading his cause with such intensity of desire that Mère Marie was forced to yield, and intercede for him with the governor. "There was nothing else to do," she wrote. "I had never believed that a savage could bear so great a love for a woman, especially a woman of another tribe." Of the Algonquin's sentiments, no word is said. We know she must have been willing to go, because she went; but if there burned in her breast any emotion to correspond with her young husband's ardor, Mère Marie makes no mention of the circumstance.

Four companies of the regiment of Carignan-Salières were left to garrison the Canadian forts when their commanders, Tracy and Salières, returned to France. A number of soldiers received their discharge, and remained as settlers, being well pleased with the beauty of the country and the freedom of the life. Each of them was given land on which to build a home, and goods to the value of one hundred livres. Each of them, if unwedded, was promised a wife when the next shipment of young women reached Quebec. The importation of marriageable girls had been going on for some years. As early as 1654 Père le Mercier makes mention of eighteen maids, brought from honest and respectable families, "for we will receive no others," who came under the care of a nun from Quimper, Mère Rénée de la Nativité. By 1666 the numbers had greatly increased. The *Journal des Jésuites* records the arrival of a ship from Normandy having on board one hundred and thirty farmers and artisans, and eighty-two young women of good character, fifty of whom had been trained by nuns in Paris.

The principal sources of supply were at first the homes and asylums where orphan children had been cared for since infancy; but it was soon discovered that country girls, accustomed to farm work, made the most helpful wives. "Experience shows," wrote Mère Marie, "that no others fit so well or so happily into these surroundings." They were drawn from the large families of small farmers, were selected by the curés of their respective parishes, and were well content to hazard a new life, a strange country, and an unknown husband. It was something to be called the "king's girls," by which name they were known, and it was more to receive from the royal purse a small dowry, usually the equivalent of eight months' provision. Talon required the applicants to be healthy, free from any repulsive disfigurement, and provided by the curé or by a magistrate with a certificate of good behavior. Colbert wrote to the Archbishop of Rouen, asking him to charge the priests of his diocese with the task of looking up country girls who were strong enough to bear the cold of New France, active enough to help with field work, good enough to make helpmates for decent young colonists, and adventurous enough to be willing to cross the sea."

Great care was taken of the prospective wives during the voyage. They were put in charge of a matron paid by the king for her services. Mme. Bourdon brought several convoys of girls to Quebec; Marguerite Bourgeoys looked after those destined for Montreal; and we read in the *Histoire de la Colonie Française* of a Demoiselle Etienne who in 1671 was paid the sum of six hundred livres for keeping watch and ward over the girls sent from French convents to Canada, and for seeing that they were safely married. It is estimated that in twenty years no less than a thousand young women were despatched to New France "*pour peupler le pays*," which duty they amply fulfilled.

It was inevitable that amid such numbers of assisted emigrants there should have been some "mixed goods," to use Mère Marie's telling phrase. A favorite jest among the loose-tongued was that Paris ridded herself of prostitutes by marrying them to colonists. La Hontan, writing after Talon had been recalled, permitted himself some witticisms on this subject; but La Hontan always preferred a *plaisanterie* to a sober fact. His book is entertaining, and its illustrations are truly delightful. There is a picture of a beaver of such ferocious aspect that it would have struck terror into the hunter's heart, while its house of mud and sticks bears a striking resemblance to the catacombs. But the author could not see his way to being both accurate and amusing, and he preferred to amuse. As a matter of fact, every reasonable precaution was taken to exclude women of loose lives from the lists. We have Colbert's word for it, and Colbert's word counts for more than La Hontan's. "The utmost care was exercised," he wrote, "in the selection of colonists for New France. When girls were sent over to be married, their conduct was rigidly examined, their stories and their circumstances were well known. Moreover their good behaviour as wives and helpmates was a proof of the success of the system."

The system *was* successful. There is no doubt about that. It proved the correctness of Dr. Johnson's axiom that the majority of marriages would be as happy if the Lord Chancellor made them. Not an atom of romance entered into Canadian wedlock, unless indeed it happened that a man and a maid felt a mutual attraction for each other at first sight. The girls sent to Quebec were housed in the Ursuline convent, and presented *en masse* for inspection. The habitants looked them over, "like cattle," La Hontan said. But the chosen girl, unlike the chosen cow, was free to say "No" if she did not fancy her suitor. Questions and remarks were exchanged. The young man asked the young woman where she came from, and to what kind of work she was accustomed. The young woman asked the young man what was his occupation, if he had a home to take her to, and how was his farm stocked. So sure were the colonists that these would be the first queries, that when a ship was expected they made pathetic efforts to have what Mère Marie calls "*une petite établissement*" ready and waiting for the much-desired wife. She tells us also that no sooner was the ship sighted

than they hurried to the convent, eager to get a
first glimpse, and, if possible, a first choice. As
it had to be a final choice, it was naturally a
matter of importance.

It was well that the habitants were ready and
eager to marry, for Talon had no mind to permit them to remain single. The Jesuits' sympathetic regard for bachelorhood was necessarily lacking in a man whose one idea was to
populate the country. Courcelles shared his
views, and both were subject to vigorous prod-
dings from France. "Those who refuse to marry
should be made to bear the heaviest burden of
taxation," wrote Colbert sternly; "and it would
be well if some especial mark of infamy could
be added." In 1668 the king enjoined Laval to
do all that lay in his power to promote early
marriages. A royal fund was established which
gave to every youth who married before he
was twenty-one a bonus of twenty livres, and
to every girl who married before she was seventeen the same uncompensatory sum. Munro
quotes a list of fifty young couples each of which
received from this fund a gift of fifty livres.

As for infamy, Courcelles could not well
brand the unmarried colonist as a felon, or weld
an iron collar around his neck; but what he

could do, he did do. When a boatload of girls came to port, the few recalcitrants—and there were very few—were told to choose a wife within a reasonable time, or forfeit the right to hunt and fish in the woods. Parents who neglected to arrange marriages for their children were fined. The affluent were not exempt from the performance of this great duty. A few fairly well-born, well-bred young women were sent from France to marry officers and colonists of standing who could not find wives among the daughters of their friends. Mère Marie writes more than once that the supply of girls is exhausted, and that Quebec is waiting for more.

It was made clear to all these newly wedded couples that they were expected to increase and multiply, which they did. In 1660 Laval was able to report that the colonies were growing rapidly because the women of New France bore more children than did the women of old France, and because more children lived—"maladies being rare." In 1668 he wrote to M. Pointevin: "Our French colonists have very large families; eight, ten, twelve, and occasionally fifteen and sixteen children. The Indians, on the contrary, have as a rule but two or three, and very seldom above five."

Incentives to paternity were not lacking. Bounties on babies—on an excess of babies— were offered by the governor in the name of the king. A man who had ten children born in wedlock received a pension of three hundred livres a year. A man who had twelve children received four hundred livres a year, no insignificant sum for the time and place. Mère Marie comments again and again on the size of the families and on their sturdy health. "It is astonishing," she writes, "to see so many good-looking, well-built children. They run around bareheaded, barefooted, with only a little shirt on their backs, they live on bread, and sagamité, and eels, and they are hardy, big and bold."

Père Dollier de Casson, most intrepid and most humorous of priests, wrote to France that while the Canadian climate was generally invigorating, women throve in it better than did men. They had large families of healthy children, and themselves remained buxom and strong. Aubert, who made a more careful study of conditions, had little but good to report. "The colonists of New France," he wrote, "are vigorous men, well-made, nimble, and self-reliant. They are always ready for war, and capable of enduring great fatigue. They are born in a good climate, are sufficiently nourished, and accustomed from childhood to physical exercise, hunting, fishing, and canoeing."

It probably sounds better than it was, like the Happy Valley, and Merrie England, and the Golden Age; but certain requisites for human content are visibly present in the picture. Men were perforce self-reliant when they had no one but themselves to rely on. They could not send around the corner for anything they chanced to want, so they looked ahead and provided for their own needs. They were, in the main, free. If constrained now and then, as in the matter of marriage, such laws were in accord with normal human desires—not in fanatical opposition to them. The colonist was poor, but then no one was rich. He did not know the bitterness of contrast, the unfathomable gulf between plutocracy and penury, the perpetual vaunt of wealth he might not share. His life was hard, but had in it no element of servility. "Poverty," said Bossuet, "is no evil to men who derive from it a sense of independence and liberty."

Chapter XIII

THE FRUITS OF VICTORY

THE successful termination of the Holy War changed the face of New France. Peace meant expansion, and expansion meant a more exacting civilization, a higher standard of comfort, and a notable increase in internal bickering. Being less occupied with the iniquities of hostile savages, the colonists had more leisure in which to find fault with one another. Public affairs did not then mean news to be read unconcernedly in the morning paper; they meant matters which touched individual habitants very closely, improving their circumstances or increasing their taxes as the case might be. Laval candidly admits that the king spent much on the colonies and got little from them. His interest was great, his generosity excessive; but, being Louis the Fourteenth, he was fundamentally incapable of allowing the colonists to manage their own affairs in their own way. On the liberty and the capacity to do this has depended the ultimate well-being of every New World settlement. Courcelles and Talon were aware that Canada was being kept too long in leading strings, and an Ursuline nun shut up in a convent on the hill came to the same conclusion. Having studied the new rules for regulating commerce, for preserving order, and for raising revenues, Mère Marie observed thoughtfully: "It all sounds well, and begins well; but God alone knows how things will turn out. We have learned from experience that the results of law-making can never be foreseen."

The oppressive sense of danger had been lifted from men's hearts, or rather had been shifted from the hearts of the colonists to the hearts of the Iroquois where it did them a world of good. So fearful were they of a fresh invasion that, according to Père Dollier de Casson, every tree and every bush appeared to them a Frenchman. Mère Marie writes that savages who had hitherto felt themselves masters of the wilderness now spared no pains and certainly no promises (they had always been liberal in the matter of promises) to secure peace. "They are humbled to the dust."

Missionaries were sent to them, among others François de la Motte-Fénelon, a Sulpician, and a cadet of the illustrious house of Salignac, the glories of whose past were to be revived in the brilliant and popular Archbishop of Cambrai. The Abbé Fénelon bore no resemblance to his famous relative. He had received minor orders in France, and had been ordained in Quebec. He went from one remote post to another, living for years among the Indians, and maintaining amicable relations. Always silent, he grew more and more taciturn. We owe most that we know about the aborigines of New France to the freely related experiences of the missionaries. "Sagacious and keen," says Parkman, "with faculties sharpened by peril, they made faithful report of the temper and movements of the distant tribes among whom they were distributed." Fénelon was an exception to this good rule. His reports were brief, his comments negligible. When Laval begged him to tell at length the tale of his adventures, he replied: "Monseigneur, the greatest kindness you can accord me is to spare me from talking about myself." When Mère Marie, abandoning the abstract for the concrete, asked him how he managed to live for so many months in the year on an unbroken diet of sagamité, he said that he had ceased to think of food in any other terms. A remarkable answer, and a no less remarkable frame of mind.

A tide of something which the modest minded

might have called prosperity poured in upon Quebec. One of the outward semblances of wealth, currency, was fast displacing the cumbrous system of bartering goods. According to Mère Marie, Tracy and his troops were largely responsible for this change. "Money is now common," she writes. "The French officers brought a great deal of it to this country, and the soldiers paid in cash for everything they bought." Trade with the Indians was conducted as it had always been, and the farmers still exchanged their produce for household goods. Among the plain people a little coin went a long way. They made what they required. This was a matter of pride to Talon, who wrote to Colbert that he could clothe himself from head to foot in Canadian products: homespun cloth, homespun linen, homemade leather, and all of them good. Only a pioneer people knows how many things it can do for itself, and how many more things it can do without. Mère Marie tells her son that four years will turn forest into farm, and that the grazing land is better than any that can be had in France; but when her sister desires seeds and bulbs of Canadian flowers the nun is amused at the notion. The flowers of New France, she explains, are as wild as the natives. They are not planted in gardens. They spring from the generous soil.

As Quebec developed, Mère Marie's letters reflect every phase of the development. She writes less and less about the things of the spirit, and more and more about what is going on around her. No wonder that she is the often quoted authority for the *Histoire de la Colonie Française en Canada*, published in Montreal in 1866. Its author, Abbé Faillon, meant this work to be a comprehensive record of New France from her first beginnings to the English occupation; but only three volumes of the proposed twelve were ever written. The narrative closes in 1675; and embracing as it does the period of Mère Marie's activities, it makes such good use of her letters that it seems at times to hang upon her words. Her concern for the colony was deep and lasting. She was as much interested in a new brewery, a new tannery, a new market-place, as in a fresh supply of livestock sent by the king to the farmers. She tells us that M. Follin has been encouraged by Talon to manufacture two much-needed articles, potash and soap; and that the householders of Quebec have been taken to task for not having their chimneys properly swept, at a cost of six sous a chimney. Like a good economist she is delighted to record that New France, which had for so long been dependent upon imports with only beavers to offer in exchange, has now a line of exports. Three ships were chartered in 1670 which carried white pine, fish oil, salted eels, and dressed hides to the West Indies, sugar from the West Indies to France, and commodities of all kinds from France to Quebec. "And this triple commerce is completed in a year."

To Talon is due the credit for all commercial development. He simply could not bear to see the poverty of a country teeming with potential wealth. It was he who built the big brewery in Quebec, partly because the colonists spent too much money on French brandy, and partly because Colbert approved of malt liquor; "for by reason of the cold nature of beer, its vapors rarely deprive men of the use of their judgment." It was Talon who vowed that New France, which had hitherto raised little but rye, should, before he was done with her, send wheat to Europe, which prophecy was actually fulfilled.

Montreal shared in the general well-being. Once sure of her life, she began to reap the fruits of her superb situation. Indian traders came from the great lakes, and *coureurs de bois* brought their spoils to this accessible colony. The year after the Holy War, two splendid adventurers, Radisson and Groseilliers, brothers in arms and as shrewd as they were daring, reached Montreal with a fleet of canoes, three hundred Indians, and a cargo of furs worth two hundred thousand livres. It was the rich result of several years spent in the wilderness, and was quickly disposed of. Neither of these typical wanderers cared to linger longer than was needful in the haunts of civilization.

The weekly markets established in Montreal, in Quebec, and in Three Rivers stimulated traffic. Everything that could be bought, sold, or bartered was brought to them for inspection: tobacco, produce, pelts, lengths of cloth, and clumsy homemade shoes. A cask of salted eels, holding five hundred, sold for thirty-five or forty livres. A marketable hog was worth ten livres more. Butter brought from twelve to sixteen sous a pound—a costly luxury. In her content with the improved circumstances of the country, Mère Marie would even have us believe that the officers left in charge of Tracy's new forts had rather a good time, which could never have been their way of thinking. "They clear the land," she wrote in 1667, "and live well, having plenty of cattle and poultry. The rivers and lakes are full of fish, the forests give them game. Passable roads have been made from one fort to another. These gentlemen have married Canadian wives, and have built themselves comfortable homes."

There was no lightening of Mère Marie's labors as her years drew to a close. She had mastered the Huron, Algonquin, and Iroquois tongues; but it had taken the hardest kind of study. "I could not have dared to fancy myself teaching our little Indians in their own speech," she wrote. "Yet by the grace of God this is just what I am doing." She was by no means vain of her accomplishments; but her carefully cultivated humility was not proof against the comments of friends who said that the task could not have been so very difficult inasmuch as she had mastered it. This neighborly line of reasoning she declined to accept. "A great desire," she protested, "will carry one far. I would force my soul into my tongue to make it utter the words I wish to speak."

Speaking was, however, only one of many requisites if her work was to outlive her. For a

number of years she instructed the young nuns
in the Indian languages so that there should be
a supply of trained teachers. For their use, and
for the use of her little savages, she wrote simple
catechisms in the Huron and Algonquin tongues,
a sacred history and a collection of prayers in
Algonquin, a catechism and a primitive dic-
tionary in Iroquois. Even to friends this must
have implied a fair amount of toil. Mère Marie
was by nature a daughter of Mary. All mystics
are. She would fain have sat at the feet of Christ
in blissful quiescence and contemplation. But the
rôle of Martha had been assigned her, and she
ennobled and sanctified it.

In one regard the letters of this observant
woman grow less sanguine with increasing years.
She had begun, just as the Jesuits had begun,
by hoping and believing that the Indian could
be permanently civilized. After long experience
she came to see that he was not a savage by
chance but by nature, and that he offered an
adamantine resistance to the processes of civilization. The marvelous adaptability of the negro, who fits easily into "the ringing grooves of
change," had no counterpart in the North American Indian. Savagery, civilization, slavery, freedom, ignorance, education——the negro has ac-

cepted them all, and has thriven on them. The Indian led his own life, or he died.

Mère Marie's letters to her son are filled with accounts of the natives, both children and adults. His interest in them seems to have been unending, and his conception of them cynically clear. In answer to his doubts as to whether the Huron and Algonquin converts were *aussi parfaits* as primitive Christians, she admits that they were neither polite nor very agreeable, and that their intelligence, though keen, had been trained along especial lines. But she insists that they understood the truths and followed the practices of religion. When the sailors or colonists sold them brandy, they became drunk and violent. On recovering, they did penance at the church door, being forbidden to enter for two or three days. Their behavior was like that of a child sentenced to stand in a corner. These penances were imposed by the elders of the village, who were more severe with the culprits than the missionaries thought it wise to be.

Mère Marie echoes the Jesuits' praise of the modest fashion in which the Indian women dressed. She greatly admires the ornaments made of porcupine quills, some of which were colored a deep red, "as beautiful as the cochineal dyes of

France." She gives an amusing account of the puzzled awe with which the braves regarded a letter. They would carry one from Quebec to a remote village, and listen "in ecstasy" when it was read aloud to them, and they recognized the accuracy of the news. "They could not understand how a scrap of paper could tell so many things and never be mistaken."

The passion of the Indian for gambling gave genuine distress to this level-headed nun who had been used all her life to thrift and wise expenditure. Other vices were more degrading, but no other was so inherently futile, and no other took so tight a grip upon its victim. The savage had little to lose, but that little was his all. Charles Fox would have been considered a very ordinary gamester in the woods of North America. A bowl of bark and some black and white pebbles, in lieu of dice, constituted the simple outfit. With its help the young brave risked his tobacco, his ornaments, his weapons, his wife, his blankets, beavers, moccasins, and whatever else he happened to possess. Reduced to nakedness, he wagered his hair, which, if he lost, was cut off and burned; and a finger or two which were severed from his hand, though of no earthly use to the winner. It must be said for him that if he was the worst of drinkers, he was a model gambler. He never permitted himself to show the slightest annoyance when he lost, nor any exultation when he won. The jubilant laughter of the successful and highly civilized bridge player would have seemed to him indecent and ill-bred.

Mère Marie considered that the few Iroquois children who had been sent to the convent were more adroit and intelligent than other little Indians, but also more impatient of restraint, and more prone to melancholy if restrained. "They love their liberty," she writes, "and their values are different from ours. Nothing in their eyes is of any worth that does not relate to war or to the chase." Here and there in her letters are charming and very modern touches. She describes the small savages marching in a self-constituted procession round and round the *crèche* at Christmas time, carrying little torches of bark because candles were so dear. She hears an Indian mother say to her children who were fearful of being left in the convent: "If when I was your age I could have had such a chance to be tended and taught, I should have been only too glad to go to school." Which proves that in a world of seeming variety and of undoubted change, parents are, and have always been, generic.

Very little is said in Mère Marie's correspondence concerning her French pupils. To learn about them we must turn to other letters, or to an occasional paragraph in the *Relations*. One of the early editors, Abbé Ferland, who was Laval's great friend and champion, grows eloquent on the subject. He refers again and again to the inestimable advantage it was to Quebec to have, even in her hard and primitive days, a group of women who could give her children the rudiments of education, and train them "in the purposes and niceties of life." The historian, Sulte, says much the same thing in his *Histoire des Français Canadiens*. He finds the Ursulines to have been sufficiently well educated "to keep intact the accent, the vocabulary, and the general tone of good society." It was due largely to their influence that the amenities of social contact were preserved in the families of Quebec. Ferland and Sulte are reinforced by Mr. C. W. Colby in his *Canadian Types of the Old Régime*. "Apart from its insistence on religion," he writes, "the convent education aimed at preserving purity of speech" (the beautiful speech of Touraine), "at inculcating courage, and at humanizing the pupil through the medium of such polite accomplishments as seemed suited to the needs of a young country. From the outset the nuns identified themselves with the land."

This identification was complete. As the years went by, Mère Marie chose Canadian novices in preference to French ones, simply because they would not "miss France." We know that in 1669 the pupils paid one hundred and twenty livres a year for board and tuition. In addition to their studies, which were probably very simple, the little girls were taught "*les ouvrages de goût*," which meant fine sewing, embroidery, lace making, and perhaps painting—or what passed for painting in the convents of that day. The nuns made the church linen, and found time amid their many avocations to embroider handsome altar cloths, and to paint "two pieces of architecture to match the Tabernacle of the parish church"—a somewhat cryptic statement. They also learned—indefatigable women that they were!—to copy the precious wampum; and we read in the *Histoire de la Colonie Française* that the collar of beads given by the governor to Garakontié was made in the convent, and was both "big and beautiful."

Ferland had as keen an admiration for Mére

Marie as had Tracy, and he knew a great deal more about her. He judged her qualities with an impartial eye, and paid a just tribute to her life's work. "At the head of a community of women," he wrote, "and devoid of resources, this remarkable nun inspired her companions with the courage and the absolute trust in God that animated her own soul. If misfortunes came, she met them with composure and steadfastness. Always tranquil, she would neither be stayed by fear, nor swept to excess by zeal. Her thoughts were clear, her style correct, her judgment firm."

Perhaps the constraint of zeal cost this devout soul more than did the banishing of fear. She was not wont to be afraid, and she disliked exceedingly to hear the petty discomforts and the semi-occasional perils of her life exaggerated by those about her. She found no hardship in plain living, and she resolutely declined to think herself in danger when she was not. But no one could have better understood the inadequacy of fleeting emotions, even the noblest, as a foundation for endeavor: "In our transient enthusiasms," she wrote to her former superior at Tours, "we naturally and unconsciously think more of ourselves than of the objects we face.

When this first ardor weakens, our tendencies and inclinations remain on the ordinary plane of life."

To have learned such a lesson without resentment and without discouragement is to have climbed one pinnacle of Christian philosophy.

Chapter XIV

THE DAWN OF A NEW DAY

IT HAS been said very often and very truly that men and women who shut themselves away from the world are not best fitted to train the young for contact with the world. But the barriers which divided the Ursulines of Quebec from the closely knit society about them were so flimsy as to be for all practical purposes non-existent. The nuns did not go into the town, but the town came to them. They knew, not only everything that happened, which was not much, but every conflicting purpose which helped to keep the colony in a turmoil. Mère Marie, whose interest was unflagging, took pains to be well informed. Her reputation for sanity kept pace with her reputation for holiness. If she believed too readily in the first report that reached her, she did not cling obstinately to an early conviction in the face of later evidence. She was on more intimate terms with Courcelles than with Talon. The intendant, who had a quick and lively disposition, found little to attract him in her grave bearing and direct speech. He liked better to go to the

Hôtel Dieu, where a brilliant French nun, Mère Marie de la Nativité, charmed him with her grace and wit.

The jurisdiction of New France was clumsily contrived, and was administered in the interests of the litigious; but it did not stand for tyranny or oppression. The governor, the intendant, and the council, which had been called "supreme" until Louis changed its title to "superior" ("supreme" being a word which he reserved for his own use and benefit), ruled the country. There were at first five, then seven, then ten councilors, including always the bishop. They did not work together very amicably, and they wrote as many complaints to Colbert as he would tolerate. Their salaries were too small to tempt cupidity, and fees were strictly prohibited; but the post was an honorable one, the gift of the king, held as a rule for life, and occasionally inherited by a son. The advantage of the system was that it left no room for "planks" or "platforms," for currying the favor of constituents, or for making preposterous promises unlikely, if not impossible, of fulfillment.

A pioneer community is necessarily democratic. Adam delves and Eve spins, and there is little room for the gentleman. The seigneur did his best to play a gentlemanly part, and he had all the outward semblances of rank. His pew in the village church was as wide, as deep, and as decorated with armorial bearings as though he had been a British squire. Special prayers were offered for him in the pulpit, as though he had been a member of the royal family. He walked next to the officiating priest in processions; and everybody waited after Mass until his carriage had gone bumping down the road; if he had a carriage, and if there was a road. He was also buried in the church instead of in the churchyard—a coveted privilege.

Seigneurs only might be ennobled; and the desire to belong to the *noblesse* was so strong among the plain-living landholders of New France that the king was both amused and exasperated. He said that they kept too many horses and too few cows; and he expressed a fear lest, having no money on which to support their high pretensions, they might become robber barons as in the Middle Ages—if only there had been some one rich enough to rob.

Opposed, though in no unfriendly fashion, to the aristocratic pretensions of the seigneur was the very real dominion of the farmer and the trader. On them Canada depended for her daily bread, and very often for the chance to eat that bread in safety. Soldiers defended the towns and trading posts, but countrymen defended themselves. Every Sunday afternoon, save in midwinter, they were drilled in the use of arms. The captain of the local militia was appointed by the governor. He was less imposing than the seigneur, but of more practical importance, being responsible for the security of his neighbors. He might be peasant born, but he was empowered to raise the flagstaff—emblem of royal authority—before his door. He was necessarily a man of sagacity and of cool courage. He illustrated in his homely fashion the proud words of Froissart, who had small thought of farmers: "The kingdom of France was never brought so low as to lack men ready and willing for the combat."

The methods by which information was conveyed to the public made for democracy. Ordinances were read aloud at the church door after Mass, and all important news was retailed in the same fashion. The congregation, which had no Sunday paper, was thus posted on matters social and political, and it discussed them

at leisure before going home to dinner. Every
man learned what his neighbor thought, and
popular opinion was slowly solidified, a word
and an idea at a time. That axiom of old France,
"It is best that people should not be at liberty
to speak their minds," was unknown in New
France. More than once taxes were readjusted
to meet the reasonable demands of farmers who,
having made up their minds, spoke them with
decision and despatch.

Justice was harshly administered. When Pierre
Boucher—he who boasted to the French king
that he had one hundred and fifty living de-
scendants—was asked if Quebec were a law-
abiding town, he answered sternly, "We know
how to hang in Canada." One could wish that
the first culprit to learn this bitter truth had
not been a girl thief of sixteen; but in pioneer
communities theft is a grievous offense. The habitants, who had not as a rule a lock on their doors,
depended upon one another's honesty, and this
was a matter of pride as well as of convenience.
The principal sources of danger were the sailors
in port, and the soldiers left behind by Tracy
to garrison the forts. Mère Marie tells a dreadful story of a friendly Iroquois chief, Sonnon-

touan, who was robbed and murdered by three soldiers of Montreal. They plied him with brandy, killed him in his drunken sleep, hid the body, stole his valuable furs, and sold them, which sale led to their undoing.

It was a crime fraught with danger to Montreal and to New France. It struck a blow at the friendly relations between the French and Indians, and it threatened to destroy forever the red man's confidence in the white man's word. Courcelles lost no time in indecision. He hurried to Montreal, called together the Indians, Iroquois and others, made them a brief, stern address, repudiating the deed with horror, and ordered the three murderers to be shot then and there before the assembled throng. "This appalling spectacle," writes Mère Marie, "did more than appease the followers of Sonnontouan. It seemed to all the savages an excessive punishment. Only one Indian had been killed. Why should three Frenchmen die? This was not their conception of justice, and they tried to prevent the triple execution, saying that the death of one soldier was enough to expiate the crime. Courcelles replied that by the law of France all were guilty, and all must die. After the sentence had been carried out, he restored the stolen furs to the family of Sonnontouan; and the Indians dispersed, deeply impressed, and more than a little terrified."

Talon, who, although masterful, was the least quarrelsome of men, tried hard to restrain the habitants from litigation; but many of them came from Normandy, and the Normans have always been wedded to lawsuits. The story of New France is one of strangely blended inhumanity and kindness, of quarrels and friendly deeds. There was constant friction between the clericals and the council; but the governor sent fresh fish to the Jesuits twice a week during Lent, and they repaid him with jars of olives, when they had any. The citizens of Quebec could see without concern a girl of sixteen hanged for stealing; but when the wife of Jacques Fournier was prosecuted and fined for humorously libeling an unhumorous acquaintance, the fine, at the intercession of the governor, was turned over to her children, so that the jester was none the worse for the sentence. Dueling was not uncommon among the officers, and on one occasion two of Mère Marie's outdoor servants undertook to settle their differences "after the fashion of gentlemen." They seem to have been inexpert swordsmen as no

injury was done to either of them; but the harm-
lessness of the diversion failed to justify it in
the eyes of the indignant nun. On the other
hand, when the house of Guillaume Bance, a
poor man, was burned to the ground, fifteen of
his neighbors helped him to rebuild it, working
even on a holiday for this good end.

In their dealings with the red man, the nuns
imitated as closely as possible the methods of
the Jesuits, who, while teaching the truths of
Christian doctrine in their very simplest forms,
forebore to outrage the sensitive pride of the
savage, or to disestablish customs which usage
had endeared to him. The structural complete-
ness of Christianity made no impression on his
mind; but its emblematic side attracted his
curiosity, and ritual won his heart. He had em-
blems and ceremonies of his own, and was
familiar with these avenues of approach. An Indian woman who feared that her baby, born in
the forest, might die before it was baptized, hung
her rosary around its neck, so that the good
Lord, recognizing the symbol of faith, might
know that, although unchristened, it was a
Christian child.

Everything was done to enhance in savage eyes
the dignity and desirability of faith, and no op-

position was offered to the simplicities of an abandoned heathenism. A Huron girl, who died in the hospital after baptism, was buried with all her most precious possessions, beaver skins, moccasins, and beads, so that her relatives might not be outraged by seeing her go naked and un-adorned into the spirit world. An Algonquin squaw, long held captive by the Iroquois, was sent with her six-year-old daughter to Quebec after the Holy War, and was there instructed and baptized. Much was made of the occasion. "His grace the bishop officiated," writes Père Dablon, "and Mme. d'Aillebout" (widow of the "insanely pious" governor) "stood godmother to the woman, who was christened Louise. The child was named Marie Anne. The Ursulines, to whose care she has been confided, say that she is a very intelligent little savage. M. Talon provided a feast which followed the cere-mony."

It has been well said that the Jesuits who made the first Indian converts had a firm grasp of kindergarten methods long before the days of Froebel. Their teaching was an ingenious, strenuous, highly developed object lesson. Every-thing had to be presented to the savage intelli-gence through the medium of his senses. He measured and appraised the unknown by the known, applying to all problems the rules and tests with which he was familiar. Hence his never-failing confidence in the efficacy of noise. He knew that it terrified the enemy. He had been frightened by it himself. Therefore he used it as a remedy for illness, and as a protection from storms, floods, and earthquakes. Wherever evil influences were at work, noise might drive them away. The same method of reasoning induced an Indian woman to refuse baptism because she was too old to undertake a journey to Heaven. She had back of her a lifetime of long and hard migrations.

The missionaries learned all that they knew by experience, and if experience be the best, she is also the costliest of teachers. Père Dablon, rejoicing in the unbroken peace of 1669 and in the new missions opened that year, observes thoughtfully: "The Iroquois are always Iroquois, and the Algonquins are always Algonquins. It behooves us to keep both in the straight path, the first through their fear of France, the second through their wonder and admiration. The haughty and superb Iroquois must moreover be handled with great care, *and spared the humiliation of being thought to fear.*"

Père du Perron, who did not lack adjectives, said that the Indians in their native state were "patient, liberal, and hospitable; but also importunate, visionary, childish, thieving, lying, deceitful, licentious, proud and lazy." Of these superabundant demerits, childishness was the most difficult to control. A good man may approach a bad man with some basis of understanding ("there, but for the grace of God, goes John Bunyan"); but the wisest of men is at a loss before the vagaries of an undeveloped intelligence. Mère Marie, enlarging on this theme, tells the story of an Iroquois brave who was hunting in the forests when he dreamed that he had murdered his wife. This meant that murder her he must. It was inconvenient that she was at the time a matter of ninety leagues away, in a village outside of Montreal; but a duty so imperative took no count of distance. The husband covered those leagues, growing more and more indignant, no doubt, and more and more murderously inclined, with every weary mile; reached the village, and smashed his way into the hut where the woman was hiding. The frightened creature climbed into the loft, leaped through a hole to the ground, and ran to the nearest neighbor for protection. "Dreams have great credit here," is the nun's composed comment upon the incident.

The year 1670 was a significant one in the history of New France. The winter was exceptionally long and severe. "In the thirty-one years we have been in Quebec," wrote Mère Marie, "we have never before known such cold. All our pipes were frozen hard, and the absence of water gave us plenty of exercise. We tried at first to melt the snow, hoping that this would suffice at least for our live stock. But the supply proved inadequate, and there was nothing for it but to have the oxen drag all we used from the river. The poor beasts were nearly ruined going up and down the steep and icy hill. Now in June the snow still covers our garden, and many of our trees are dead. The whole country has suffered greatly. The hospital nuns are especially to be pitied, for they have lost one of the finest orchards in the land."

This was the first winter that La Salle spent in the inclement wilderness. This was the winter that Louis Joliet and the two Sulpicians, Père Galinée and Père Dollier de Casson—who always came in for adventures—lived in a trapper's hut on Lake Erie, hidden by snowdrifts from the world. This was the year recorded in the *Histoire de la Colonie Française* as pregnant with promise for the future. The Iroquois who came in ever-increasing numbers to trade in Montreal had described two mighty rivers which they often confused with each other. One they called Ohio, which meant beautiful, and the other Mississippi, which meant great. It was the hope of reaching these rivers, and discovering through them a route to the Orient, which induced La Salle to abandon a profitable seigneury, and become a great explorer. In the same year, 1670, this interesting note appears in the *Relations:* "We" (the Jesuits) "have resolved to send an expedition to assure ourselves of the truth regarding the generally accepted belief that by means of the river called Messipi or Missisipi we may reach the sea of Japan, and facilitate commerce with the east."

La Salle's party was organized on a large and imposing scale. "So greatly did M. de Courcelles have at heart the success of this expedition," writes Abbé Faillon, "that to insure its safety and lend it importance he permitted soldiers to leave their companies, and join the ranks of the adventurers." They set out with high hopes; and Talon's secretary, M. Patoulet, made this formal announcement of their departure: "M.

La Salle and M. Dollier de Casson, accompanied by a number of brave and hardy men, have left New France with the design of discovering a waterway which will enable us to reach Japan and China. The enterprise is difficult, the result doubtful. God grant it the hoped-for success. There is one good thing to be said: His Majesty the King has not been called upon to pay the expenses of an undertaking which may come to naught."

Chapter XV

THE CHANGING SCENE

In the autumn of 1671 Mme. de la Peltrie died of pleurisy. Hers had been an interesting and in many respects a noble career, full of sharp contrasts, and upheld by a high sustaining purpose. A brilliant, impetuous, ardent woman, fertile in expedients, she had carried her point against heavy odds when she resolved to devote herself and her fortune to the Canadian missions. She had been a true and tried friend to the Ursulines who knew her worth, and to their Indian protégées who mourned her deeply. She had not only kept faith to the end, but she had preserved to the end a large measure of her early enthusiasm. If she lacked the serenity and the illumined common sense of Mère Marie, she was none the less a very gallant lady, and Quebec was left the duller, as well as the poorer, for her loss.

Her reluctant suitor and loyal friend, M. de Bernières, had died in 1660. His last years had been spent in the seclusion of the Hermitage, a retreat which he had established at Caen for devout laymen who wished to live in peace, unvexed by the problems of the world, or by women who made the world so problematic. Here he was surrounded by a group of young men, among whom at one time was Laval. Here he defied his growing blindness by dictating several religious books, all deeply tinged with mysticism, and with that pleasant but fruitless quietism then rife in Spain and France. One of them, *L'Intérieur Chrétien*, went through many editions. Its author had traveled far since those stirring and harassing days when he helped to dupe M. de Chauvigny, and establish the Ursulines in Quebec. His nephew, Père Henri de Bernières, administered the last rites of the Church to Mme. de la Peltrie; and Père Dablon, writing for the *Relations*, exhausts himself in pious rhapsodies over her saintly life and death. It is the fault of such commentators that we fail to glimpse the real woman behind this torrent of laudation.

That there was a very real woman, vital to her finger tips, and possessed of the resourcefulness as well as of the inconsistencies of her sex, no one can doubt who reads her record, or looks upon her portrait. The daughter who outwitted her father, the widow who pressed into her service a man of influence and authority, the enthusiast who stood ready to sacrifice the pleasures of a very pleasant world, the inspired leader who chose Mère Marie out of a convent full of nuns to do the work for which she was so eminently fitted, the sanguine, devoted, willful *fondatrice*, who was so uncertain yet so profoundly reliable—hers was a character worthy of something better than an indiscriminate and edifying eulogy.

Abbé Casgrain, who deals habitually in superlatives, is no more enlightening than is Père Dablon. He does devote some pages to Mme. de la Peltrie's personal charm, to her good looks and winning manners; but for the rest he takes cognizance of nothing that is not supernaturally perfect. She must have been very lovely in youth, for her portrait painted in middle age is full of life and *espièglerie*. The face is round, the forehead broad, the eyes are bright and glancing, the lips full and sweet. The semi-religious costume is dignified and very picturesque. The hands are folded decorously as though in prayer; but the side-long look beneath the narrowed lids is faintly amused, and the mouth is ready to smile. It is said of Saint Catherine of Siena, who Heaven knows had plenty to depress her, that

she was "always jocund and of a happy spirit."
Mme. de la Peltrie was plainly of a happy spirit;
an impulsive, gay-tempered creature, immaculately free from the ostentation of wealth, and
generously interested in all that went on about
her.

Why such a woman should have habitually
alluded to herself as the most depraved of sinners
might puzzle a biographer, did we not recognize
a custom common among pious mortals whose
sins are not worth considering. The higher a
soul advances in grace, the clearer must be its
consciousness of imperfection, the wider grows
the gulf between aspiration and fulfillment. This
was what made Laval say with his last breath:
"They were saints. I am a sinner." This was
what forced from the dying Saint Theresa the
reiterated plea: "Remember, Lord, I am a daughter of Thy church." But self-accusation may be
a mere *façon de parler*. When Mme. de la Peltrie
denounced herself as a vile and abject wretch,
or as the most unworthy creature in the world,
she knew that she was nothing of the sort. She
was not practising humility, she was not yielding
to vanity. She was repeating a formula of old
and good standing. It had no significance whatever.

When we pass from words which are the daughters of earth to deeds which are the sons of Heaven, this lady, who was neither saint nor sinner, leaps into vivid life. The evidence of her contemporaries is clear and convincing. Of all the group of women who sailed for Quebec in 1639 she alone had left a life of luxury, she alone had come straight from the ways of wealth to the ways of poverty, from pleasant idleness to hard, unlovely work. All agree that she did this work, not in the spirit of sacrifice, but with eager interest and desire; and not for a few months, but for many years. Happily she was too well-born, too sure of herself and of her lineage, to think any kind of labor degrading. She did not have to make acts of humility where she saw nothing humiliating. She scrubbed the floors, the pots and kettles, and the Indian children with equal vigor and thoroughness. Her perfect health defied cold, fatigue, and sagamité for thirty-two years.

Mme. de la Peltrie's supreme accomplishment was sewing. With skillful fingers she fashioned endless garments for the little savages; and, once they had been taught to keep themselves tolerably clean, she took delight in making their dresses neat and well fitting. Apart from the invaluable income which she brought to the convent, she was of great service, and always an agreeable and well-bred companion. When she took the bit between her teeth, and fled to harder and more exciting conditions in Montreal, Mère Marie never lost confidence in her return. When she tried to take the bit between her teeth, and fly to the well-nigh unbearable conditions of a mission outpost, the missionaries with equal confidence turned her back to Quebec. As the years passed over her head, these restless impulses no longer stirred her heart. The impetuous spirit was sobered, the keen mind grew tranquil and perhaps a little torpid, and Madame la Fondatrice became *"la douce et pieuse dame"* whom Laval commended, and for whom Talon had a just regard.

One curious bequest she made on her deathbed, and she made it apparently at the request of the Jesuits, which seems more curious still. She directed that her heart should be taken from her body, enclosed in a plain, unpolished wooden box, and buried beneath the altar step of the Jesuit church, in fulfillment of a promise made to the priests. Her wishes were reverently carried out. When her remains were laid to rest in the choir of the convent chapel, her heart was interred under the step of the high altar in the church of Notre Dame des Anges. The painting that hung above this altar, the silver lamp that swung before it, had been her gifts. She had now, in all reverence and simplicity, added a third.

It must be remembered that in the Seventeenth Century the heart had not been degraded to the important but strictly utilitarian office it holds to-day. Much romance was still attached to it, and the custom of disposing of it in an elaborate and troublesome fashion had the sanction of age and authority. The far-traveled heart of the Bruce, which never reached its destination, is the most notable case in point. Another is the heart of that superb soldier, Bertrand du Guesclin. A third is King Edward the First, who directed that his heart should be sent to the Holy Land under the care of one hundred knights, who were to guard it on the way and remain in Palestine, fighting, if need be, for a year. His unworthy son found this behest to be difficult of fulfillment, so decided to ignore it altogether. He buried his sire intact in Westminster Abbey, forgot his example as quickly as he had forgotten his command, and went headlong to disaster.

Mme. de la Peltrie's death was a grievous

blow to Mère Marie. It broke the last link with France, and with those bygone days now obscured by three decades of hard Canadian life. The mere sight of this early associate must have recalled the lost loveliness of Tours. The mere sound of her voice must have brought back the polished utterances of Touraine and Alençon. Mme. de la Peltrie was moreover a highly educated woman according to the standards of her day; and a knowledge of the world had taught her much. Who among the younger nuns, or among acquaintances in Quebec, could fill her place? Charlevoix is right when he says that mutual interests and common experiences had bound together these two disparate souls. When Mère Marie watched by the bedside of her dying friend, she must have called to mind that eventful day in the convent of Tours when the charming young widow (or was she a wife?) came to choose a superior for the Canadian mission. She remembered no doubt the ecstatic hope with which the nuns had regarded a visitor who bore such a gift in her hands; the assurance of her own soul that she would be chosen, the throbbing of her heart when Mère Françoise de Saint Bernard told her that she was free to go. Half a lifetime had sped by since then. She was older than Mme. de la Peltrie, and the years were crumbling beneath her. It was not a parting of the ways. They were nearing the goal together.

Nothing so accentuates the flight of time as changing conditions. Tours in 1671 was probably the same Tours that Mère Marie had left in 1639; but Quebec was not recognizable as the rude little town which had welcomed her so warmly, and housed her so indifferently, thirty-two years before. Even the half-dozen years of Talon's administration had witnessed great results; but Talon was admirably fitted to alter the face of the earth. No grass grew under his feet, no air became stagnant about him. He was essentially a bureaucrat, a man to deal with men. An alert and practical intelligence sped him on his way, a trained discernment took careful count of obstacles. Overshadowed by the greater figure of Frontenac, he has been somewhat neglected by the historians of New France; yet turn where we will we see his hand at work. Tenacious and indefatigable, he lost sight of nothing that could advance the prosperity of the land.

Such a man knew well that the Company of the West Indies was stifling Canadian trade, and he probably suspected that it was headed for bankruptcy; but in this regard he was powerless. The theory of monopolies was deeply rooted in the hearts of kings; and the only relief that Talon could devise (a good measure as far as it went) was to manufacture more, and buy less in France. If his dream, like the dream of Champlain, was to conquer the frozen North, he understood the greater possibilities offered by the West and South. There ran the great unknown river, for the discovery of which he paved the way; there lay buried the mineral wealth he coveted (among his gifts to Colbert was a lump of pure copper which came from the shore of Lake Superior); and there were the English, strong and unfriendly, the enemies of France in the Old World, and her rivals in the New.

Talon was not by nature a pacifist, but he knew that quarreling was a waste of time and strength. Canada had to check the hostility of Indians, and to conquer the hostility of Nature. Her hands were full, and she needed more than did other colonies the strength that lies in union. There was no love lost between the governor and the intendant, which was natural when their authority overlapped. Courcelles held the higher office; but Talon was styled Intendant General of Justice, Police, and Finance in New France, which covered a good deal of ground. Courcelles said that Talon ignored him, and Talon said that Courcelles condescended to him. Both men were probably right; but neither permitted his personal rancor to affect their public intercourse, or to interfere with their mutual labors.

Again it was natural that Talon, as a Gallican, should have been opposed to the authority of Laval, and to the overwhelming influence of the Jesuits; but he knew the value of both. For Laval he had a reluctant admiration. A nobly born churchman who upheld the dignity of his office and ruled his flock austerely, yet who made his round of duties on snowshoes, or kneeling for hours in a canoe; such a man was a colonist after the intendant's own heart—prelate and pioneer. As for the Jesuits, he made good use of them. He believed them to be better acquainted with the savages than were other habitants, and more sincerely their friends. Therefore he commissioned them to send him reports from outlying posts, to keep him informed as to the temper of the tribes, their movements, and the volume of trade to be expected from them.

The advancement of New France under

Talon's stimulating care is faithfully recorded in Mère Marie's letters to her son. Mr. James Douglas, in his scholarly study of Seventeenth Century Quebec, says that these letters are "more valuable as sources of contemporary history than are even the Jesuit *Relations*. They describe simply but graphically all that occurred in the community. They were not meant to edify the devout, or to move the charitably disposed." This is a great point in their favor. Mère Marie was a paragon of beggars; but she did not beg from her son because he was a monk and had no money. For the same reason there was no call to edify. She does indeed ask his prayers that she may become "a holocaust on the altar of God's glory in whatever fashion He deems best"; but for the most part her letters deal with her surroundings rather than with herself.

There is something pleasantly ironical in the relations between this mother and this son. She had left him in his boyhood, and had not seen him since his twenty-second year. He had become, after a somewhat turbulent youth, a satisfactory and fairly scholastic Benedictine of the Congregation of St. Maur, and was of sufficient distinction to have his life written, printed, read, and forgotten. When she was old and he was middle-aged, many letters passed between them. He afforded a natural outlet for the human part of her which had been steadfastly repressed. What he wrote about we do not know; but it is evident that the correspondence was an abiding interest in his life; for if her letters were delayed by a pressure of work, or by irregular transportation, he sent anxious queries and protests, to which she replied soothingly as a mother would, and with many promises of amendment.

If Quebec forms the background of Mère Marie's letters to Dom Claude Martin, she has also much to say concerning the missions and the missionaries. She writes about the experiences of Père Pierron among the Iroquois, who practised hospitality and grew excellent pumpkins, but were exceedingly hard to convert. She was well acquainted with Père Dollier de Casson, that picturesque giant of a priest who had been a cavalry officer under Turenne, who was the most popular chaplain in New France, and who, being rudely interrupted by an Indian when he was at prayer, knocked the intruder down without rising from his knees, or interrupting his devotions. She describes admirably the comet of 1668, "shaped like a lance, of an angry red color, and with a tail so long that it was lost in space." And now and then she sends her son an Indian curio like the drum of a medicine man.

It was the changing aspect of her adopted country which filled Mère Marie's mind during the last years of her life. She sensed the importance of the new day, but she knew that her night was at hand. Maisonneuve, who should have died where he had lived so valiantly, had been recalled to France. Talon was soon to go. She at least was left to end her days in the scene of her activities. There stood the strong gray walls of her convent, there lay her garden walks, her cultivated land. There too were her young nuns, her French pupils, and the long, orderly file of little savages. When she went home she would take her wages in her hand. She looked at the fast-growing town about her, and felt that she had been part of its growth. She looked at the widening river, and remembered the words in which it had been described to her: "beautiful as the Seine, rapid as the Rhone, and deep as the sea." She thought of that other and still greater river for which search was being made. Anchored fast, her mind flew far afield. Her keen curiosity was unmarred by personal restlessness, or by personal desires. She was where she was by the will of God. Did she perchance read Thomas à Kempis, and learn from him the value of quiescence: "What canst thou see anywhere that thou dost not see here? Behold the heavens, the earth, and the elements. Out of these are all things made."

Chapter XVI

MYSTIC AND EXECUTIVE

The image of Mère Marie which lingered long
in the mind and heart of Quebec was that of a
tall, sedate, comely woman sitting under a giant
ash tree in the convent court, and instructing
a little group of Indian, or perhaps of French,
children. It is a pity there is no portrait of her
extant. To know how she looked would help us
to interpret her character. Mme. de la Peltrie's
portrait is very revealing. So too is Talon's with
its débonair beauty, its fire and foppishness, its
gayety and resolution. The Sieur de Sillery's,
on the other hand, is the embodiment of asceticism, modified by a meticulous air of breeding.
Even Marguerite Bourgeoys has come down to
us in a sketch as charming as it is characteristic.
Her sidelong glance is less intimate and smiling
than Mme. de la Peltrie's, her nose is middle
class, her mouth firm and well cut. Her dress,
with its carelessly tied hood, its pointed collar,
its cross worn as an ornament, is a triumph of
artistic simplicity.

But of Mère Marie we have nothing that is

authentic. After her death, Courcelles commissioned a local artist to make a sketch of her wasted face; but even that was lost in the second fire of 1686. The pictures which commonly accompany her biographies are confessedly "drawn from imagination." One of them might be called "Portrait of a Nun," and the other "Portrait of a Nun at Prayer." No real woman ever looked like either. We have the assurance of Charlevoix—who never saw her—that her features were regular, but of a masculine cast which suited her grave manner and unusual height, that her voice was agreeable and her carriage dignified. He adds that her constitution was good (it needed to be), and that, while her manner inspired respect, no one was ever embarrassed in her presence.

The seventeen months that followed Mme. de la Peltrie's death were the least eventful that Mère Marie ever spent in Quebec. Peace reigned, the colony grew slowly, and Frontenac had not yet crossed the sea. In her convent all went well. If, as she wrote a year before her death, they were richer in spiritual than in temporal wealth, that was as it should be. Her own words vouch for it: "To be stripped of possessions, and of the desire for possessions, is a lovely thing. A disembarrassed heart is happy." Nevertheless there was no dearth of food, or fuel, or clothing, or candles for the altar, or of alms for the savage poor, who were now infrequent visitors. Mère Marie alone remembered the days when hungry Indians emptied the pot of sagamité, and the nuns went supperless to bed.

The health and vigor of this model pioneer were unfailing until her seventy-first year. Then they broke, and the activity, though not the usefulness, of her life was over. For months before she died her sufferings were augmented by the ruthless remedies of her day. Charlevoix, who goes into minute details without making clear the nature of her disease, tells us that the abscesses in her side were burned deeply with caustic. She bore her pain quietly, attended to the business of the convent as long as she could, suffered her chamber to be crowded with visitors (dying was not then considered a private affair), and, when the end drew near, bade farewell to her pupils, both French and Indians, and to her sorrowing nuns. It is said that the joy she felt in dying illumined her dead face, and it was little wonder. Her work was done, her hurts were healed, and home was close at last. She looked so supremely happy lying dead on her narrow couch that the mourners dried their tears and rejoiced. It was no occasion for grief.

Quebec gave its much revered nun an august funeral. All the notables attended it, and Père Lalemant made the indispensable oration. No business was done that day. Men called to mind the dead woman's life: her coming, the enthusiasm with which she had been received, and her long years of labor. They said to one another that a chapter of history was closed; and that if her work survived her, it would be because of the spirit she had infused into her fellow workers. That the nuns felt for her affection as well as deference does not admit of a doubt. "That tenderness in austerity, and that austerity in tenderness," which Baron von Hügel says is the "very genius of Christianity," were manifest in all she said and did. Her habitual silence was neither sad nor repellent. Her unalterable evenness of temper was but the reflection of her undisturbed serenity of soul.

Francis Parkman, while admitting Mère Marie's intelligence, and her supreme executive ability, accuses her of "an enormous spiritual pride." It is a grave accusation, and one as difficult to refute as to prove. Spiritual pride is doubtless visible to the eyes of God as are all our other sins; but it is a trifle hard for us to distinguish it by the light of ordinary evidence. Perhaps the old counsel, "If we would really know our hearts, let us impartially review our actions," is as good a rule as we can find; and, judging by her actions, Mère Marie's spiritual life was sound to the core. Saint Gregory says that humility of soul is the mystic's safeguard. Mère Marie was at all times a mystic; therefore it behooved her to be humble. Parkman had the profound distaste for mysticism that was characteristic of his generation. He pronounced it "insane," which is a satisfactory definition of any phenomenon of which we disapprove.

Charlevoix, dealing with this enigmatic but supremely important phase of Mère Marie's life, is both intelligible and reasonable. He quotes the rule laid down by the fathers of the Church, which says very simply that the faithful may (note there is no "must") believe that the secret elevation of the soul is by the grace of Heaven, provided that the mystic's life corresponds in the eyes of men with such a grace, and that there is no sign of self-esteem or of mental weakness. This is the common language of theologians. "The human soul has a natural capacity, but no exigency, and no positive ability, to reach God otherwise than by analogical knowledge. But God permits some souls to feel his sensible presence which is mystical contemplation. In such an act there is no annihilation or absorption of the creature into God; but God becomes intimately present in the created mind."

The danger of such individual experience is the tendency of the devout soul to become a law to itself. This is why Saint Theresa warned her nuns that they must never allow the illumination of prayer to decide for them anything concerning their duties, work, responsibilities, or routine. The rule of the order was the rule for them—and for her. Once when she was frying fish for the convent dinner a sudden ecstasy of contemplation wrapped her round. Its sweetness was overwhelming, but it did not distract her attention from the matter in hand. Her business was to fry the fish, and she fried it.

Charlevoix says that while there is certainly no obligation to believe that Mère Marie's mysticism was a genuine and a holy thing, such a belief is reasonable because there is no discordant note in her life or in her writings. "All was seemly in her behavior, all was sane in her advice." "To the fervor of the mystic," comments a recent historian, "she joined that strong sense of the actual which marked Odo of Cluny, and Bernard of Clairvaux." This was evidenced in the discipline of her convent, in the hold she had upon the rulers of Quebec, in the unfailing success with which she carried through every measure she undertook, in the temporal as well as in the spiritual wisdom of her axioms and her rules. There was in her a solidity of judgment, a clear and practical intelligence. If she habitually contemplated the heavens, she walked the earth with firm and sure steps. Moreover, she had a great and salutary regard for the judgment of others, and this is always a safeguard. Wisdom would not die with her, and she knew it.

There was no radical change in Mère Marie during the long years of her cloistered life. She met altered circumstances with altered efforts, and sometimes with an altered point of view. Her horizon widened, and her interests widened with it. Her responsibilities grew heavier, and her administrative ability grew stronger with experience. But from first to last she never lost the supreme quality of the mystic—a sense of personal relation with God. Parkman, who was much displeased with her life in Tours, and much pleased with her life in Quebec, came to the conclusion that she was a reformed character, and amiably commended her reformation. "Marie de l'Incarnation, no longer lost in the vagaries of an insane mysticism, but engaged in the duties of Christian charity and the responsibilities of an arduous post, displayed an ability, a fortitude, and an earnestness which command respect and admiration. Her mental intoxication had ceased, or recurred only at intervals; and false excitements no longer sustained her."

It is hard to think of anybody less sustained by excitements false or real than this balanced and decorous woman, who from early youth manifested the same traits that distinguished her later years. There were no doubt alternations of light and shadow in her spiritual as well as in her temporal life, moments of joy and moments of depression. Mutability is the order of existence. But at all times and under all circumstances she was self-controlled, of a still and grave demeanor, and endowed with a capacity for affairs. A poor young widow who was so useful in the conduct of business that her relatives deplored and resented the loss of her services, must have been as good a supervisor at thirty as at sixty. If there dwelt any illusions in her soul, they certainly were not fostered by idleness.

Mère Marie's letters begin with her life in New France. Before that time her compositions were purely religious, and were written either for the use of her novices in Tours, or at the suggestion of her confessor, who seems to have considered that the best way to clarify thoughts and impressions was to set them down in the lucidity of words. But when transplanted to Quebec, letter writing became an important part of her daily duties. How was she to raise money for her convent, her school, her little savages, her needy pensioners, save by enlisting the sympathies of the wealthy and distinguished? In later years, when begging was no longer imperative, she kept on writing about her adopted country because the keenness of her own interest found delight in awakening and gratifying the interest of others. There is something inspiriting in this animated concern for all that went on about her, and there is enlightenment in her carefully considered verdicts.

Take, for example, her final tribute to Argenson. Mère Marie was well aware on what grounds he and Laval had fallen out so bitterly. Her sympathy as a friend and her loyalty as a nun were enlisted on the prelate's side; but nothing could blind her to the courage and capacity of the governor. When this courage and this capacity were questioned in the dark days of Indian warfare, she championed him against all criticism. When he was recalled to France, she wrote these well-considered words in his behalf:

"M. Argenson had much to bear from discontents who censured him for refusing to risk an attack upon Quebec by withdrawing its garrison for active fighting. He saw himself powerless to protect the length and breadth of New France with the scanty forces at his command, and he could not leave the towns at the mercy of the Iroquois. He was compelled to make all decisions for himself, as he stood in need of wise and loyal counsellors. He was of a generous mind, and singularly patient under criticism. He came often to the convent, and never let pass an opportunity of doing us a kindness. We talked much about public affairs. His successor, M. d'Avaugour, says frankly that he cannot understand how the country has been so well looked after with a meagre income and an inadequate army."

The rules prescribed by Mère Marie for her

nuns were moderate, her counsels prudent and kind. She discountenanced self-imposed asceticism, having need of healthy workers, and rightly considering that the climate of Quebec, the poverty of the convent, and the restricted food supply provided all the austerity of which they stood in need. The business of keeping warm in winter time was one of supreme importance. If the braziers failed to affect the frozen chapel air, the nuns said their prayers in the community room or in bed. But if forced to endure cold, they were expected to endure it uncomplainingly, and as a matter of course. They were not the only people shivering in New France.

The one approach to impatience noticeable in Mère Marie's writings is her distaste for great talkers. Habitually silent, she forgot that many excellent and useful people are habitually talkative, and that allowance must be made for this harmless and not altogether unnatural idiosyncrasy. Even edifying speech wearied her if it lasted long. "Too many words are fatal to religious devotion," she wrote. "The heart and the mouth do not open simultaneously." A bustling haste was also little to her liking: "Our hurry to be done with one thing so as to begin another means the ruin of both." Inevitably she was drawn to contemplation as the purest form of prayer: "It is said that contemplation is idleness, and in a fashion this is true; but it is idleness alive to every impression of divine grace. The highest life consists of spiritual nearness to God and the active practice of duty." One is reminded of Joubert: "*Vivre, c'est penser et sentir son âme.*" To find time for this ennobling leisure as well as for hard systematized work is to leave nothing unenjoyed or undone.

Mère Marie was fundamentally humorless. There is an occasional caustic quality in her writings which relieves their intense seriousness. Her advice to her nuns, to "Bear with man for the sake of God," covers a great deal of ground. Her comment upon an invoice of marriageable girls, that they were "mixed goods," "*une marchandise mêlée,*" was as near an approach to humor as her letters can show. Of Saint Theresa's daring wit, of the flashing speech, keen as a blade, which distinguished Saint Basil of Cappadocia and Saint Thomas Aquinas, there is no vestige, nothing to indicate that they would have even carried a message to her mind. Her language, always unadorned, seems now and then preternaturally calm, considering the things she has to tell. She notes the death of the Mohegan captive who gave warning of the threatened invasion of the Iroquois in words so matter of fact, "after disposing of him in the usual way, that is by burning," that the baldness of the statement lends an added horror to the deed. It must be remembered that burning a prisoner of war was in the nature of a compromise on the part of the Algonquins. They could not understand the squeamishness with which the missionaries regarded the old and respected custom of prolonged torture; but they had substituted the stake as a comparatively merciful measure.

If Mère Marie's letters lack the lightness of touch which would have made them as delightful as they are informative, they are often couched in very engaging language. She writes to the superior of the Ursulines at Dijon, suggesting that, as they have but little money to spare, they might be all the more generous with their prayers: "It would be a deed well worthy of your piety to try with the help of your religious to gain a hearing from God, that He may be kindly disposed to the poor savages of New France." A gentle and irresistible petition.

Charlevoix tells two characteristic stories of Mère Marie when she was still Mme. Martin, attending to her brother-in-law's business, and filling her scanty leisure with works of charity. A poor little shopkeeper of Tours had been accused of dishonesty. Everybody save the young widow believed him guilty; and when she pleaded for him, and proclaimed her belief in his innocence, the judge reprimanded her for risking her fair name and the respect in which she was held by such ill-advised partisanship. Nevertheless the man was later on cleared of the charge; and so deep was the impression made by her courageous stand that humble folk, who rightly fear the law, looked upon her as their champion against injustice.

The other tale is of a woman, also belonging to the lower class, whose son had committed an unnamed crime, and who was wrought up to such a pitch of sorrow and rage that she passed from one convulsion of fury into another. Mme. Martin, who had been called in by the frightened neighbors, tried in vain to quiet her with kind and gentle words. The wretched mother, past all control, heard nothing, saw nothing, but shrieked and tore at herself and at her clothing like the mad creature that she was. Then the visitor suddenly flung out her strong arms and clasped the swaying woman to her breast. Close, close she held her until the beat of her own heart, steady as a pendulum, quieted the throbbing heart pressed close to it. The firm will imposed itself upon the infirm will. The frantic sufferer grew silent, passive, and pitiful. The hour of dementia was over.

It is inevitable that commentators on Mère Marie's life should compare her to that great mystic and great executrix, Saint Theresa. Père Émery, author of *L'Esprit de Sainte Thérèse*, has gone out of his way to indicate the resemblance; and Bossuet unhesitatingly alludes to the Ursuline nun as the "Theresa of the North." The comparison is, nevertheless, in kind, not in degree. Saint Theresa is one of the high lights of hagiography. Her field was wider than Mère Marie's, her task harder, her mind keener, her personality more magnetic. She has stamped herself upon the history of her church. The work of reformation was her work. She did not destroy what she undertook to reform, which is always an easy thing to do. She preserved it, bettered and purified, which is exceedingly difficult. Her figure attracts and holds attention because of her vivifying and cleansing blitheness of spirit. She possessed the quality of distinction which Matthew Arnold says "corrects the world's blunders, and fixes the world's ideals."

One may be a great poet without nearing Shakespeare, and a great statesman without rivaling Pitt. Mère Marie resembled Saint Theresa inasmuch as her piety was equalled by her capacity for work. She had the same talent for administration, albeit it was exercised within narrower bounds. Her outward life was normal, and was regulated by the rules of her order. Her inner life, noble and sustained, bore fruit in her steadfast perseverance, and in her cheerful acceptance of circumstance. She had one advantage over her prototype. She was a pioneer. She had risked what in her day was the great adventure, and she had a chance to impose her personality upon a new country and a savage people. Character is the great force in human affairs, and her reliability made her a guide in doubt and a bulwark in difficulties. What Anatole France calls "*la douceur impérieuse des saintes*" was the weapon with which she fought her battles, established her authority, and became a living principle in the keen, hard, vivid, friendly, and dangerous life of New France.

Chapter XVII

THE HERITAGE

ON THE spot where Mère Marie lived and died stands the Ursuline convent of to-day, an amazing group of buildings which, with its gardens, covers seven acres of ground in the heart of Quebec, and can be properly seen only from an airplane. Six hundred people sit down daily to dinner where once the pot of sagamité held the rations for nuns and savages. Secular residences of every kind hem in the school, the cloister, the convent chapel, the quiet walks. No one passing the inconspicuous gateway on a little crooked street would dream that here was a village set apart from the city which encircles it. Throngs of schoolgirls coming and going with much chatter and a brave array of books seem its only link with the world outside its doors.

Yet the place has one historic association which draws many visitors to this oldest convent school in North America; for here, when Quebec was won for England on the Plains of Abraham, was buried the Marquis de Montcalm, lost leader of a lost cause. The battle, so decisive in

its results, was little more than a skirmish; but
the landing of the British troops and the scaling
of the cliff—steeper in 1759 than it is now—were
triumphs of strategic warfare, and the death of
both commanders supplies the sombre note of
tragedy. Wolfe, indeed, fell in the hour of victory.
Like Dundee, he heard the exulting shout which
told him that he could afford to die because his
work was done. Montcalm fell in the hour of
defeat, knowing that with him perished the hope
of France. He thanked God that his end was
near, and that he could not see Quebec pass into
English hands. Before he was cold it had changed
masters. Brigadier Senezergues, the second in
command, lay mortally wounded. Vaudreuil, the
governor, was valueless as a leader. In the terror
and confusion of that night an old servant of the
Ursulines made a rough box of pine boards, and
carried Montcalm's body to the convent. A shell
had burst under the flooring of the chapel, making a shallow grave in which it was hastily
interred. A little group of French officers stood
sadly by. The populace wept in the streets. A
new order reigned.

Wolfe's body was taken on board a man-of-
war, the *Royal William*, and carried to England
for burial. The tiny bay where he landed his

troops has ever since been called Wolfe's Cove. The shaft raised to commemorate his deed bears a brief and noble inscription: "Here died Wolfe victorious." By way of contrast, a marble headstone erected over the grave of Montcalm on the hundredth anniversary of his death has a Latin epitaph composed by the French Academy of Inscriptions and Belles-Lettres, and containing one hundred and ninety-two words—a triumph of verbosity. His skull was exhumed in 1831. It rests in a glass case in the visitors' chapel, and on the wall Lord Aylmer placed an oval tablet inscribed:

> "*Honneur à Montcalm!*
> *La Destin en lui dérobant la Victoire*
> *L'a récompensé par une Mort glorieuse.*"

Finally, the monument which stands in the Governor's Garden overlooking Dufferin Terrace honors both leaders, and tells its tale in three compact Latin lines:

> "*Mortem Virtus Communem·*
> *Famam Historiæ;*
> *Monumentum Posteritas Dedit.*"

Quebec has no mind to have this page of her history forgotten.

After the British occupation the English governor, Murray, made the convent his headquarters, and kept the nuns hard at work looking after his sick and wounded soldiers who could not be accommodated in the hospital. The new officials were as friendly to the institution as the old ones had been; and it is worthy of note that the first superior elected under the British rule was Esther Wheelwright, who had been captured by the Abenakis when she was a child of eight or ten playing on Wells Beach, near the old town of Wells in Maine. After some years of savage life she was bought or begged from the Indians by the Jesuit missionary, Père Bigot, and brought to Quebec. The governor, Vaudreuil, received her as a ward, and placed her in the convent school, where in due time she became a nun and head of the house. There was always this natural affinity between adventure and the Ursulines. In what other convent could little girls have had the felicity of being taught and scolded by a religious who had enjoyed such terrifying experiences?

This being the case, it seems doubly strange that the Ursulines of Quebec should still be cloistered nuns. It is said that Cardinal Bégin proposed in 1919 that they should follow the example of other convents, leave their enclosure, and—education being now a complex and troublesome thing—learn at first hand what the outside world could interpret. Most of the teaching orders have for years past attended college courses, the summer schools affording profitable occupation for their holidays. The propinquity of men students has long since ceased to disturb them. In the natural order of things it should be an incentive to effort. And surely the American Ursulines who, scornful of discomfort and danger, established the Rocky Mountain missions with a dozen flourishing centres, and penetrated to Alaska when that bleak territory was purchased from Russia, had little need of grilles to separate them from their kind. Saint Ursula and her virgins were no keener to sail strange seas, and tread the far-off regions of the world.

But in the conservative atmosphere of Quebec a grille still seems a sacred thing, and no partition can be too flimsy to acquire dignity and meaning in the eyes of the enclosed nuns. To sit on one side of a latticed wall and have a visitor sit on the other side has for them a significance which is lost on the mundane guest. One wonders if Mère Marie would not have availed herself of the cardinal's proposal, if she would not have welcomed new conditions which promised new values. Her constitutional fearlessness always stood her in good stead. Her sense of the actual was too strong to permit her to confuse it with the symbolic. A rule meant much to her. It was a thing subject to change (otherwise there would be no growth), but calling for implicit obedience while it lasted (otherwise there would be no order). A groove meant to her nothing, and less than nothing. She had escaped from every groove in which she had been imprisoned by circumstance.

If it takes seven acres of convent to carry on the life work of Mère Marie and keep her memory green, there stands in the lower town, across from the tiny Church of Notre-Dame des Victoires, a hostelry called the Hôtel Blanchard. The oldest part of this building is a small solidly built house with a high-pitched roof, window boxes, and an overhanging balcony. It looks for all the world as if it should be facing the Seine, with tables between it and the river holding bread and wine and plates of black cherries— what Mr. Sinclair Lewis calls "the holy simplicities of life." This is the spot where stood the rough, strong little "Louvre" which sheltered the Ursulines for three years. A commemorative

tablet gravely records the fact. Here Mère Marie
rested as best she could after her long voyage;
and from this point she looked out upon the
river, "not yet brutalized by quays or humiliated by bridges," and knew that Quebec was
beautiful. Her certainty was shared by Père Le
Jeune and by most of her contemporaries. There
was no dissentient voice even in the town's rude
infancy. "This is an enchanted spot," she wrote
after she had surmounted the worst of her
difficulties. "The trials of life came so lovingly
that the more we are harassed by them the
sweeter is our content, and the stronger the
affection in our hearts."

"*La race Canadienne a pris racine*," says
André Siegfried; and the imperishable quality
of what was once New France is reflected most
clearly in Quebec; in the splendor of Dufferin
Terrace, studded with tourists; in the steep
steps descending into Petit Champlain and
Sous-le-Fort streets with their air of sombre
antiquity; in the moldy Quai du Roi; in Notre-
Dame des Victoires, with its battlemented altar,
and its courteous recognition of our Lady's
services in repelling the ill-mannered Phipps,
and in dispersing the fleet of Admiral Walker in
1711. "Quebec is old like old cathedrals," wrote

Louis Hémon, "like Latin prayers, like venerable relics in their reliquaries. She knows that nothing can destroy the seed which she has planted in the soil of America, and that the rapid revolutions of the New World fail to disturb the serenity which she bore like a stolen secret from the land of France."

The same understanding, the same content are evinced by M. Athanase David, Secretary of the Province: "How clearly in the turmoil of to-day is heard the voice of Quebec!" he writes dispassionately. "It is not loud, but it is listened to with attention, carrying as it does a note of peace, an echo of the common sense which rallies and directs mankind."

It is a pleasure to hear common sense alluded to so kindly, the quality being somewhat out of favor with thinkers to-day. Even Abbé Dimnet, from whom one might expect a kinder estimate, holds it in some contempt as but another name for conformity. Yet Benjamin Franklin, who stands as our best and noblest exponent of common sense, was not precisely a conformist. He was not a follower. He was a leader. He was not timid. He was fearless. By the same token, Mère Marie, toiling in her humble field, arrived at wisdom through the exercise of that un-

flawed common sense which studied circumstances, measured possibilities, took chances,
and achieved results.

While the Ursuline convent has expanded from
a hovel to a domain, Laval University has also
spread itself over a vast area of Quebec. It is a
huge medley of masonry, without perceptible
plan, yet of a curious and altogether casual
picturesqueness. Its high-flung gallery com-
mands a superb view of the St. Lawrence and
the Laurentian hills. It has steep stairways,
rambling corridors, a valuable library, and a
museum containing more bad pictures with
good names attached to them than any other
collection in the world. A stone arch marking
the entrance of a narrow passage shows a mono-
gram of three letters, S. M. E. It is that of the
Séminaire des Missions Etrangères. Laval's
little sons, their dark blue coats enlivened by
green sashes, lend color and animation to the
streets. Laval himself, the fighting bishop, has
been pronounced venerable by the Church he
served. He is en route for sainthood, though out-
stripped in the race by the eight Canadian
martyrs who were canonized in June, 1930.

The story of these eight men is familiar to all
students of American history. Parkman has

borrowed it from the *Relations*, and told it graphically. Mère Marie has told it. So has the *Histoire de la Colonie Française en Canada*. Six of the eight were Jesuit missionaries. Père Isaac Jogues, who, rescued from the Iroquois and carried safely to France, returned with freshly healed wounds to meet his duty and his death. Père Jean de Brébeuf, nobly born and the bravest soul in the Canadian wastes. Père Gabriel Lalemant, who heads all Christian martyrology as the greatest sufferer of that suffering host. Père Noël Chabanel, who had known no life save that of the woods since he had finished his studies in Toulouse, and who was but thirty-six when he was butchered on his way to the Sault de Ste. Marie. Père Charles Garnier, killed by the Iroquois at the mission of St. Joseph. He might have escaped with half-a-dozen Huron braves who urged him to fly with them; but he stayed in the flaming village to give absolution to the dying until his moment came. Père Antoine Daniel, who fell, pierced by arrows, at the door of his little chapel where he had been saying Mass.

So much for the priests. They had taken vows, and were faithful to them. But there were two others, strong young *donnés* whose business was

not the saving of souls, but the care of their
friends the missionaries for whom they laid down
their lives. One of these, Jean de Lalande, had
at least the mercy of a swift death. He was
brained by a Mohawk hatchet, and fell by the
side of Père Jogues. But René Goupil, a surgeon
of Anjou and a man of parts, was cruelly mutilated and suffered to live for several days, during
which time he dressed the wounds of his companions as well as his crushed fingers permitted.
Then an old Iroquois chief in a sudden access
of anger ordered him to be killed, and his body
was flung to the dogs and prowling foxes that
devoured it.

No study of contrasts can be sharper than that
provided by the august ceremonies of canonization which proclaimed these men to be members of the Church Triumphant, and the squalid
setting of their martyrdom. We call to mind the
vast dome of St. Peter's, the glow of color,
the glory of music, the dignified ritual and the
throngs that witnessed it; and then picture to
ourselves the foul hut where Père Lalemant,
scorched and mangled, breathed through the
long night hours, the woods heavy with horror,
the sinister sound of Indian devilry.

And Mère Marie who knew these men, and

sorrowed for them, and gloried in their glory?
She too has taken the first step toward canonization, having been declared "venerable" by
Pope Pius the Eleventh in April, 1922, the two
hundred and fiftieth anniversary of her death.
A solemn triduum in honor of the event was held
in the convent of Quebec. Twenty-two years
earlier Leo the Thirteenth had called a congress
of Ursulines in Rome. They came, these roving
daughters of Saint Ursula, from every corner of
the known and little-known world. Their mani-
fold experiences delighted the sagacious pontiff
who loved the unfamiliar. And one and all held
in deep reverence the name of Marie de l'Incarnation.

Carlyle said that a well-written life is almost
as rare as a well-spent one. Mère Marie's life was
so eminently well spent that it is hard to do
justice to its goodness without losing sight of
the fact (denied, or at least ignored, by her
biographers) that she was as human as the
militant Laval, the denounced Argenson, the
diplomatic Talon. Her ecstatic piety never ob-
literated her practical qualities. She lived for
thirty-three years amid hard, primitive, and
deeply interesting conditions; and she preserved
throughout a stable harmony with both man and

Nature. "The deep tones and slow vibrations of the seasonal earth" were part of her experience, and so too were the efforts of her countrymen to build up a new civilization in the wilderness. If she was shut up within four walls with women and children for housemates, she was in close and daily intercourse with the men who stood responsible for the welfare of Quebec. If the things of the spirit were permanent, change was the order of material life.

We are all of us the children of our time. Mère Marie believed too implicitly in tales told her by roving Indians and *coureurs de bois*, and she repeated these tales gravely in her letters. But her credulity was no greater or more unfounded than is that of the newspaper reader of to-day. In New France wanderers were the news carriers. They furnished reports, true or false, and they were listened to readily by people who had no other avenues of information. If their stories must have sometimes sounded incredible, stranger things than any they had to tell were happening daily in the forests.

The habitual gravity of Mère Marie's manner, her apparently unbroken calm, did not stand for unconcern towards others, but for the hard-fought conquest of self. Her spiritual consti-

tution had been early braced by adversity. Her
surrender of will never implied surrender of
intelligence. "*L'homme s'agite; Dieu le mène,*"
wrote Bossuet. Of this great truth she was well
aware; but it afforded her no excuse for inde-
termination. In her own domain she stood supreme and responsible. Her decisions were
supported by resources of judgment. Much of the
affection given to her was founded upon the
confidence she inspired.

Santayana says that "a certain joy and beauty
did radiate visibly from the saints." If we search
for them in Mère Marie, we shall find the beauty
expressed in order, the joy in an accomplished
purpose. Both were upheld by faith and purified
by charity, being fundamentally different from
the order and purpose of business, or law-making,
or war. "Into that great ocean to which humanity ceaselessly flows," writes Mr. Edward
Martin, "we carry only spiritual values, and
such a value is the sacrifice of one's life in the
fullfilment of a great duty." Mère Marie's life
was given unreservedly to the fulfillment of a
great duty. She saw it with clear eyes, and she
was faithful to the labor it imposed, being wholly
unafraid of what the years might bring. The
closer we look at her quiet figure, the more

firmly and nobly we see it etched against the background of history:

> Courage was cast about her like a dress
> Of solemn comeliness;
> A gathered mind and an untroubled face
> Did give her dangers grace.

Index

303